25 TOOLS FOR CAREGIVERS

SACRED DEATH

HEMALI V. VORA

Dr. Shelley Astrof, Dr. Jennifer Browne, Sherry Burns, Carol Dutton,
Theodora Elena Engelhart, Dr. Alice Feng, Brittani Frey, Robin Friend,
Kathy Guidi, Shabnam Hashemi, R. Scott Holmes, Rev Stephanie Urbina Jones,
Lisa Karasek, James Kawainui, Melissa McGlone, Jill Mollenhauer,
Kelly Myerson, Lisa A Newton, Esther Reyes, Shelley Sake, Pamela Schneider,
Dr. Krupa Vora-Knarr, Kendall Williams, Atlantis Wolf

ANICCA: IMPERMANENCE

Inspired by the impermanence of life. Life that is ever present in an endless circle of life and death and death and life.

What is the beginning of the circle? A circle, where all is existing in unity within all cosmic realities and expressions. A circle where animals, humans, plants, planets and everything beyond are part of the whole.

Infinite Transformation bringing forth creation. Humans as cyclic creatures embracing all stages of being, spiraling through the power of the elements in outer reflection to inner self revelation. Passing beyond linear time concepts into an understanding of the constant change in the ever present now.

There is a long and sacred process of birthing these collage (healing artworks). They come into being after rituals, deep meditation and intuitive nudges. As the creative energies start flowing at different hours of the day or night, I get back into that sacred space and allow the expressions to emanate into existence.

This healing artwork was created for Sacred Death book and conceptualized keeping Hemali Vora's vision for the cover in mind. And made with immense love and healing energies for all.

Theodora Elena Engelhart

www.risingroots.at

www.Instagram.com/the.common.mind

Maha Mrityunjaya Mantra
(The Great Victory over the Great Death)

ॐ त्र्यम्बकं यजामहे सुगन्धिं पुष्टिवर्धनम् |
उर्वारुकमिव बन्धनान्मृत्योर्मुक्षीय माऽमृतात् ||

Aum Tryambakam yajaamahe
sugandhim pushtivardhanam |
Urvaarukamiva bandhanaan
mrityormuksheeya maamritaat ||

Victory over the fear of death through complete surrender to the divine.

We worship the three-eyed One,
who is fragrant and who nourishes all.
Like the fruit falls off from the bondage of the stem,
may we be liberated from the cycle of birth and death.
(Very powerful chant that brings immense healing)

DEDICATION

This book is dedicated to anyone experiencing the death process in any manner, whether it's someone in the midst of their own personal journey, a family member or friend assisting a loved one, a volunteer offering their time and service, or a medical staff member whose life's work is to help others in this grand transitioning of energy into the spirit world.

The process of death, of returning home, is one of the most personal and sacred transitions we will experience in our lifetime. Through this book, the twenty-five author-experts have joined hands to share their personal experiences and expertise and offer many tools to cope with the suffering, bewilderment, grief, and despair—and to shift your perspective on death and dying. Our hope is that you find a whole new way to unravel the great mystery called death, in this book. And counter any fear or angst normally associated with the process of death and bring solace, awareness, and empowerment to experiencing or witnessing the transition.

I also dedicate this book to my dad, whose death started me on a self-discovery journey that led me to who I am today. I draw my strength from his great legacy, and I'm grateful for his continuous guidance. Love you, Dad!

To my young nephew, Abhinav, we miss you and love you!

CONTENTS

INTRODUCTION

One January 2020 morning, I woke up around 3 am to use the bathroom. After use, I turned off the bathroom light, and still semi-asleep, opened the door. I took a step back, and my eyes opened wide, my heart started racing, and my breathing got heavier. Right before me was a black, shadowy presence. Seeing me in fight or flight response, poof, it went out of my sight. It took me few seconds to realize what I saw. *Oh no, please come back; I didn't mean to get scared. Please come back, I'm sorry, I've been waiting to meet you, to see you, talk to you. Really, I'm not scared.* I waited, scanning the room and hallway to see if I would get a second glimpse if he would appear. I sat on the bed, wide awake now. *Did I really see something? Yes! Absolutely sure, it was a beautiful masculine presence. Not a doubt in my soul that it was a gentle, loving, and grand, black presence.* It was a strong knowing. Taking a deep breath, I closed my eyes; *I am really grateful that you came to visit me; I know you didn't mean to scare me. I'm sorry, but can you please tell me who you are? Your name?* And what I heard was, "Angel of Death." I was stunned.

Angel of Death, really? Are you sure? I could feel him laughing at that question. I had done countless daily meditations for the last several months, intending to know who my angel was. I wanted to know what he looked like and to have conversations with him. Finally, he came to visit me, and I got scared. *I know about Yama or Yamraj* (in the Hindu Vedic tradition, he is the righteous god or king of death, king of ancestors, king of ghosts, and king of justice). *I have heard countless stories of him since childhood. But angel? I wonder if they have an angel of death?* I couldn't fall asleep; I picked up my phone and did a Google search—angel of death. First came Azrael, Angel of Death in Islam, some Jewish traditions, and is referenced in Sikhism.

Then what I found was Top 25 Gods of Death, Destruction, and the Underworld. Gods and Goddesses from religions and mythologies—Greek, Maori, African, Celtic, Slavic, Norse, Egyptian, Vedic, Aztec, Inuit, Siberian, Canaanite, Persian, Javanese and Balinese, Mayan, Chinese and Japanese. The list was long, and I never heard of many of them. There were many ancient cultures with folklore and stories where death is openly talked about and accepted to be part of life. These were places where death and life were celebrated with the whole village or community, followed by rituals, traditions, and ceremonies during the death process and after, when a longer time was given to mourn and to be with the pain.

I wonder how and when we lost connection with the reality that our bodies are mortal and we all will die one day? When did we stop following the rituals, the home funerals, cutting the mourning and bereavement period short?

I resisted looking into it more. Meanwhile, through a few distant and in-person intuitive energy healing experiences, I had the opportunity to witness and assist with clients loved one's peaceful transitioning into the spirit realm. It was the most profound energetic, and spiritual experience ever. The Universe surely had other plans for me. Many synchronistic events led me to take End of Life Doula training.

Surrounded by fear and angst from the COVID 19 pandemic, I knew I wanted to openly talk about death and dying and, most importantly, about life and living. To replace fear with knowledge and encourage clients to create a legacy project to find their purpose. I wanted them to embrace death so they could live fully without regrets or pain. I wanted to discuss living a more aware and conscious life and educate caregivers on the importance of self-care and self-love. Finally, I wanted to talk about the transitioning stages and signs during the dying process.

When Laura Di Franco suggested the theme of the collaborative book to be on death and helping caregivers and healthcare workers, which is my passion, I was nervous and excited at the same time.

Despite many delays and fears, I knew I was continuously supported and encouraged by my guides. During my numerous daily meditations, I was shown visions of life events that connected me to death and its process. One vision was from when I was seven years old. I had an out-of-body experience when my uncle passed away. My soul floated through the rooms, all my senses heightened. It was a home funeral in India, and I observed the rituals: cotton in the nose and ears, pure, holy ganga water, and holy basil leaf in the mouth, both big toes tied. Then, wrapping his body tightly with a white cloth. The priest chanted, and family and friends were around. I noticed what people talked about, how they grieved, the rift and void of the loved ones, the heart-shattering pain, and a part of us that dies with them. As an adult, I had a similar experience with my aunt's passing.

I was also able to re-witness my dad's transition. As my soul stepped back and observed, I saw my dad, friends, and family present there, all of us surrounded and held in a bright, warm, loving light. Another meditation was a reminder of me being able to communicate and help a loved one cross over twelve days after she left her body.

My angel, the Universe, the Divine, was constantly making me see how connected I was to death and dying. From childhood and college days, where my first ever English 101 research paper was on euthanasia. How I passionately defended the dignity of the patient. Reminded of my curiosity to know what was beyond the door in the hospital rooms where hospice patients and their families were. How I used my dad's transition as an opportunity to dive deep into my pain and suffering to transform and live an aware and conscious life. And set out on a quest to find my legacy.

This book project has taken its own time, with so many shifts and changes. Each and every author was intuitively drawn or called to be on this journey. The vision took on a life of its own, propelled forward by the Divine embrace of our universe.

You do not have to be a healer to have experiences similar to those you will read in the various chapters. Anyone who has assisted a loved one, friend, or patient through the death process has most likely come into contact with some or all of the transition stages. Without the knowledge of what they are experiencing, the events are often dismissed. Many find themselves doubting what they saw or felt as they accompanied loved ones through the process, felt the feelings in the room, or noticed the sensation of the spiritual visitors. They may have noticed a shifting movement of light or the coincidences of how things and timing worked out.

In this book, our purpose is to offer perspectives to help the caregivers who are witnessing their loved ones move through the death process or grief. The authors have worked through grief in productive and inspiring ways. Some have looked for ideas in ancient times and cultures to move through pain and suffering. I hope you resonate with one or a few of the authors, their stories, and the tools. But it's not our intention to impose our vision on you. Death is personal, private, and one of the sacred processes we encounter. As we explore the death process, we must also understand life.

And to live fully, allow yourself to become vulnerable, authentic, real, and transparent. It's okay to ask for help, to delegate, to step away from it all for a while. It's okay to say no. Don't be afraid to feel and express all your emotions. Do it your way, unapologetically. Give yourself permission to grieve, mourn, and take care of yourself. Taking care of yourself is not selfish. Remember, there is no wrong or right way to move through grief. Death changes life. Be gentle with yourself and others as you learn this new being you are becoming.

Holding you in love and light.

Hemali

SPECIAL NOTE TO THE READER

ABOUT THE HEALING CRISIS

There's something in the healing world that is known as the healing crisis.

A healing crisis is a temporary worsening of symptoms that arises as we go through the healing process. It's a form of awareness I'd like you to know about as you dive into these pages. It happens when we feel the energy of an old injury, pain, or past trauma as it's coming up to be released or healed.

Initially, a process of awakening can feel terrible. We might want to retreat and shut down again. But, as much as we want to push the pain away, the body often tries to communicate to us through uncomfortable sensations and feelings.

Sometimes we ignore our bodies' messages and, in doing so, we numb our senses. Over time, unaddressed imbalances become an illness.

When any imbalance has been in place over time, it's common to feel helpless, powerless, overwhelmed, or numb. We might not believe there is anything we can do to change our situation.

That resistance comes up in you in the form of thoughts, sensations, feelings, emotions, and sometimes memories that don't feel good.

Notice your habitual reactions to them. Sometimes it's exactly what you have the most resistance around (words, ideas, practices, conversations, etc..) that are the biggest opportunity for healing. Skilled healers recognize this and assist their clients through it with tools such as dialoguing, energy work, hands-on practices and modalities, and mindset and awareness coaching.

The healing crisis and your own resistance are each an opportunity to go a layer deeper. They are doors to release and relief. And sometimes, it feels so bad you think you'll die. So please know that we (author-healer-experts) get it. And we're here for you. Healing is possible.

If you purchased this book, you'll enjoy access to a very special Facebook group called Sacred Death Community at (www.facebook.com/groups/512670289951676), where our author experts are hanging out to help answer your questions and provide you with live training. This is an incredible benefit. Make sure to take advantage of it, especially if you're stuck or have questions about what you're feeling. You're not alone. We're here to help you. Your questions will be welcomed, and your concerns will be honored. You'll have a safe space to do this work of healing.

Having said all that, know that the experts here have shared their heart-shattering stories, tools, practices they've used, and knowledge with you with a sincere and generous intent to assist you on your healing journey.

We want you to know all people are welcomed to read and embrace *Sacred Death*. We hope it will assist you and every reader through loss and the healing process.

Would you like to meet the authors and learn more about their amazing perspectives and the work they do? Please join the Sacred Death Community on Facebook (www.facebook.com/groups/512670289951676) and contact them with any questions you may have about the techniques or information they provided. They'll be happy to assist you further!

CHAPTER 1

CONSCIOUS LIVING AND DYING

CONNECT WITH YOUR HIGHER SELF, YOUR GUIDES, AND YOUR LOVED ONES USING GUIDED MEDITATION

Hemali Vora, MPT, End-of-Life Doula

It was a chilly, snowy January night. I leaned against the sliding glass door of the ICU room, looking in, scanning the room. The lights were turned off, but light from the parking lot pierced through the glass window. You could see the flurries outside and some beautiful snowflakes were sticking on the glass and melting. Loud machines beeped, some mimicking a heartbeat, and some sounding an alarm for vitals going below normal. I was very comfortable with them; I was in my element, a familiar space and place.

I walked the hallways and rooms of this hospital as a floater physical therapist for the past three years—just never at night. I treated patients and interacted with families on that floor many times. This night was different. Tonight, my dad was in that room, motionless, wires and tubes all around and on him, a machine breathing for him. This felt different. I'd never seen him like that. His health was deteriorating very fast. Four months ago, he was diagnosed with Pulmonary Fibrosis. Just last month, he was prescribed oxygen at home and diagnosed with pneumonia today. This is exactly what I feared. Just yesterday, I was yelling, screaming, pleading, and even threatening him in hopes of trying to stop him from going to work with his portable oxygen tank in freezing temperatures. He insisted on going to work. "Why are you so stubborn? Why aren't you listening to me? It's so cold; you'll get pneumonia!"

But here I was, moving around the ICU room, restless with a constant feeling of uneasiness, sometimes standing by the window and at times just standing close to the bed observing my dad. A million thoughts raced through my mind, recreating every moment of the last 48 hours. The day we argued, I flew to Vegas with my cousins, only to return the very next day after hearing the news of him being vented in the ICU.

Still standing by his side and looking at him, I was lost in thoughts. *I wanted to say so many things to him. Tell him how much I love him.* Unfortunately, all I could say out loud was, "Dad, I'm here. I'm right here. Don't worry. Everything will be okay." All of a sudden, an overwhelming feeling of love came over me, and all the emotions welled up from deep inside. *Thank you, Dad. I truly appreciate all that you have done and sacrificed for me. I am sorry we didn't really talk much lately. I'm just busy, overwhelmed, overworked, exhausted all the time, just burned-out. Once he gets better, I'll make it a point to talk to him. Tell him how I value all he has taught me. Thank him for always believing in me and for loving me unconditionally. I apologize for being upset and saying some harsh things I shouldn't have.*

Suddenly, I was aware of a strange feeling of energies with glimpses of shadows moving around us. I brushed it off, *I'm seeing things and I need to sleep.*

The next morning, he was in the same condition. By now, friends and family, local and from out of town, started pouring in. Some were praying, some were reading scriptures in the room, and some waited in the lounge. We just finished talking to his doctor about his wishes for a Do Not Resuscitate order and donating his body to a medical facility. Later that afternoon, I straightened his left leg after seeing it in an awkward position with his knee bent. He took his last breath surrounded by friends and family within 15 minutes of me trying to make him comfortable.

Tears flowing down my face, I whispered to the ICU nurse, "I killed my father. I just straightened his leg. His left leg looked so awkward, and I just wanted to make sure he was comfortable. I do this all the time before I leave my patient's rooms. I make sure they're lying comfortably in bed, with pillows tucked under." Trying to keep her composure, she replied, "You know that's not true; his body was trying very hard, he was given very strong meds to maintain the blood flow, and the machine was breathing for him. Even if he survived, all his fingers, toes, and feet would be necrotic." Deep down, I knew this, but somehow I had it in my head that I single-handedly managed to kill my dad just by moving his leg.

All of a sudden, my world stopped. That moment of utter heartbreak echoed in my soul. We all were in shock and disbelief and felt numb. Since Dad's body was donated and taken to a medical research facility in Pennsylvania the same day, there was no closure. There was no viewing, no funeral, but a small thirteen-day Hindu ritual and ceremony of last rites. Everything felt unfinished. For a few days, we were surrounded by friends and family praying and taking turns bringing food, but then came a February 2010 snowstorm that kept everyone in their homes for close to a week. This, in turn, postponed the prayer ceremony at the temple but gave us time to spend with family to support each other and contemplate life and death.

It was great to have my maternal uncle and cousin come from India. We talked about life, death, and beyond. They explained our family beliefs in-depth, especially the celebration of life. Death is part of life; we come into the world, play our part, follow whatever our purpose may be, and depart, never forgetting to pray with devotion and do Seva (service). But when it's time to go, nothing and no one can change that moment. With utmost faith and belief, we are and will be well cared for by our Divine on this earth and beyond. We're so blessed by our grandparent's and ancestor's merits and virtues that it will not only ascend us, but our generations to come will continue to reap the benefits.

As they say, life moves on. After a few weeks, family and friends slowed down and eventually stopped reaching out. Then reality hit, and floodgates of anger, loneliness, anguish, pain, and heartache became unbearable. I started to dissect every moment, hour, day, and week. I questioned myself: *what could I have done differently? How else could I have helped or stopped this untimely death?* I was descending into a spiral—the feelings of guilt and regret of not doing enough set in. And there was the ultimate guilt of killing him.

I was constantly angry with random mood fluctuations, which affected my near and dear ones. The sad truth is until you go through the death of someone you're close to and dearly love, you can't understand what grief is and how complicated it is. It surely is not a "one size fits all" experience. There are as many scenarios as there are people. At times even getting out of bed and showering was a herculean task. There were times I'd watch TV aimlessly until dawn. I drowned myself with food, work, and kid's activities. All these distractions were in an attempt not to feel the pain. I bottled it up and filed it in the locked cabinet in my mind. Anytime a feeling started to escape, I stuffed it back in, so I didn't have to deal with the sadness and heartbreak.

My siblings and mom were dealing with their grief on their own, none of us sharing about our innermost painful feelings, just good, happy memories and thoughts of what Dad would say. We all were grieving separately, smiling, and being strong for each other, just like society tells us to. This left us so lonely in our own worlds, making us believe that asking for help or crying out loud was weakness or would create more pain for others. I was very lonely for a while and filled with depression, guilt, regrets, fears, anxiety, anger, and insomnia.

I was getting sick and was exhausted mentally and emotionally. I wanted to change my circumstances. That's when I decided to look back at dad's journey and his legacy. This was a turning point in my life. I wanted to know what my legacy would be. *What's my purpose in this life? How will I make a difference? Do I matter?* I had an existential crisis. I knew it was time to take care of myself. I decided to take responsibility for my life, be aware and make conscious choices without regrets. I started taking time for myself and invested in my well-being. I got certified in Usui Reiki and joined a holistic nutrition school. I took daily walks in the woods, sat and meditated by the stream, did breathing exercises, ate well, and explored the idea of death.

I started to understand the importance of funerals, holy rituals & ceremonies and how important it is to grieve and experience the cleansing and release together. I also realized the immense power of prayers, mass prayers and in experiencing every emotion by all men, women, and children for our health, healing, and well-being. At the same token, I came to understand the power of accepting, surrendering to what is, forgiving and that there is no shame in asking for help. As a caretaker, learning to be a graceful receiver is critical. I'm grateful for the few friends who came alongside and simply hurt with me without me asking. They let me talk and cry and ached along with me. Sometimes just the presence of someone familiar brings so much comfort. After that, I made it a point to be aware of my presence, thoughts, spoken words, actions, and inactions.

My daily reiki meditation practice, well-balanced nutrition, soul food, and movement helped me heal and continues to help me live life to the fullest, more consciously. Part of my self-care is to remind myself, "You can't give what you don't have. Fill your cup and let it flow, and give from your overflow. You are more than enough; you are perfect the way you're designed; forgive yourself." I was guided to create healthy boundaries and space for myself to be authentic. Step by step, I was led through the healing process, unraveling and unveiling all the hidden pain and trauma for me to heal. All I had to do was have faith and patience, trust the process, and follow my intuition, nudges, signs, messages, and synchronicities. My mom always says, "There is always a reason for everything; there is a grand design, divine plan, and divine timing at work at all times, way beyond our control and plans." That knowledge has helped me so far on my path. Over the years, I've learned to listen deeply with unconditional positive regard, seeing all, including myself, with the eyes of unconditional love, compassion, and kindness.

One meditation, in particular, in January of 2016. After I turn on some music, lie down, close my eyes, take some deep breaths, and relax my whole body, I went off into the deep abyss of my being. Within seconds, a heart-wrenching sob emerged, screaming from my soul, mouth open, with no voice coming out, tears flowing down my face, snot through my nose. It was a full-blown tantrum with the desire to flail my hands and legs. *I want you here, your presence, in the flesh; I want to hold you tight, hug you, talk to you. I want you to be here to see, play, talk, and guide your grandkids. You would have absolutely loved them, and they, you.* Almost an hour and a half later, I calmed down. I felt a great release; finally, six years after my dad's death, I embarked on my grieving process. I stopped hiding behind distractions and stayed with the emotions and feelings, all the messy ones too.

All grief is complicated, very messy, and hard. Give yourself permission to feel everything, to go through it and not around it. Remember, with immense love, there is immense grief. The thing about grief is, there is no set date and time for the start and finish. We will continue to love, miss, and grieve our loved ones until our last breath. Suffering is an opportunity to transform, shift, and change our perspective. It's a chance to see things differently, to see life and death in a different light. Life can be as hard and painful as we make it or as loving and easy. And death is really about life and living until the last breath we take.

After that, I became very curious and looked for mystery in every experience and encounter, even for a second. I considered every experience as bringing me messages, as a teaching moment. I felt like I was on a treasure hunt, an adventure. The topic of death and dying excited me. It was only after I embraced Dad's death that I started living, experiencing the magic and miracles in every intuitive nudge and moment.

I now explore and learn verses from ancient Hindu scriptures, the Vedas, Upanishads, and Bhagavad Gita, that teaches us about death, life, living, self-realization, and liberation. I now realize that death is like going home, merging with the Divine. And we are home no matter where we are in body or spirit. We're always at home.

THE TOOL

Whenever you're ready to delve deeper, I invite you to embark on a visual meditation journey. Sit in a sacred circle. Find a comfortable, quiet, safe space. If you want, burn incense, sage, palo santo, or use a diffuser with an essential oil that calms you or brings joy. Put on some relaxing meditation music.

You can physically create a circle with flowers, leaves, stones, or crystals and sit in the center. Or you can simply visualize yourself in a circle wherever you are. There is no wrong or right way, and you don't need anything but a safe, quiet place.

For the audio meditation visit:
https://www.youtube.com/c/HealingCorner

- Close your eyes, take a couple of deep breaths, relax your whole body as you breathe out.
- Imagine you're in a beautiful grove of trees.
- In the grove is an ancient stone circle; you go and sit in the center.

- This is the sacred circle created just for you. It's a place of healing, strength, power, and wisdom.
- You can hear the sounds of nature, the birds, the breeze, the nearby stream, the humming of Mother Earth.
- A mist forms that heralds the arrival of your angels, guides, ancestors, your whole counsel.
- One by one, they appear in a circle around you. Each brings their blessings, light, love, healing, and guidance.
- You thank them for coming and journeying with you through this pain.
- Sit and place your hands palms up, resting on your knees; you're open and ready to receive all their light and healing energies.
- Feel the beautiful, bright, expanding light pour over you and encircle you. Sit in it as long as you wish to.
- It's okay if you don't feel anything or see anything. They are there around you. Hold the intention and pray.
- Give yourself permission to be in stillness. Allow the thoughts to move through. Remember to take deep breaths now and again. If needed, you can place your right hand on your heart and left on your belly. Breathe out the building stress, and release and let go of whatever is coming up.
- When you're ready, invite your loved one in the spirit world to come to sit with you in the circle. Imagine them sitting right in front of you, holding your hands.
- Don't hold back. Give yourself permission to cry, remove the armor, and open your heart. Allow yourself to go deeper into the pain. Be with the experience; remember you are in a safe protective circle. You are held, loved, and supported.
- He/She is as eager to communicate with you as you are with them.
- They want to say to you that they are surrounded with beauty with peace, and joy. They are more than okay. There is no suffering or pain. They are well taken care of.

- They want to tell you that everything is going to be okay and to move forward. They want you to be happy, enjoy and experience life, go on adventures, and meet new people. How they wish you could see how beautiful and enough you are. They are grateful for all you have done for them and ask for forgiveness if they have wronged you in any way. And now they are creating space for you to say whatever you want to say to them.

- Tell them how you feel, how angry you are, tell them everything unsaid.

- Talk to them, tell them how much you miss them, love them. How you want them to be here in person and not in spirit. How it's hard to go on or be without them. Tell them how sorry you are. Let all the emotions come through. (Sob, kick, scream, cry, foam at the mouth, tears covering your face, or even snot. Be with it all).

- Be in this moment with them, in the circle as long as you want to.

- When you're ready, thank them for being in the circle with you. Thank your angels, guides, ancestors, and all that came to the circle.

- Start coming back to yourself. Take few deep breaths, wiggle your toes and fingers. Then, come back to where you are. Be in this sacred space of love as long as you need.

Feel the release and the calmness. Remember, you are always surrounded and held in protective light. If you wish, you can journal about your messages and experience and meditate whenever you're ready to again. Not every meditation experience will be the same. If you are ready to dive deeper, it's my honor to step into the sacred space with you. You can reach me: hemalivora1@gmail.com and www.hemalivora.com.

Love and Light.

Hemali V. Vora, MPT, is an expert holistic practitioner, intuitive energy healer and a spiritual mentor. Her mission is to empower healthcare workers and caregivers towards radical self-care, unconditional self-love, and reclaiming their power. She guides them to their unique legacy blueprint by tapping into their inner wisdom and living an aware life. www.hemalivora.com, www.facebook.com/coachhemali, www.instagram.com/_happy_healthy_u

Please refer to page 213 to read more about the author.

CHAPTER 2

LIVING AND DYING ON YOUR OWN TERMS

HOW TO MOVE THROUGH FEAR, GRIEF, AND LOSS AND LIVE FULLY

Shabnam Hashemi, BSN, RN

MY STORY

"Live! Just live!" my beautiful sister Nassim said, holding my face in her hands. Those were her last words to me as she faded into sleep in her hospice bed, hours before taking her last breath. It was 2013. She had just turned fifty.

We had lost our father in 2009, which was a huge blow to our nuclear family of five. His death was sudden, leaving us little time to adequately prepare or say proper goodbyes, except for the short period he was in ICU. Along with my mother, there were three of us then, three sisters. Nassim had been battling breast cancer for four years by the time our dad passed. Just as no parent should have to bury their child, no oldest sister imagines she'll be the one guiding her youngest sister to the other realm.

Nassim generally blazed her own trail in everything. She had a pioneering spirit and would find something that she believed worth pursuing - whether food, treatment, a person worth listening to, or a course worth taking. After she would do some digging, she would share her findings, sometimes insisting that we join her in whatever endeavor she was on. She treated her cancer journey that way and kept a close diary of her progression through the years as she learned from the disease. As her favorite singer Frank Sinatra would say, she did it her way. She hoped her diary would help others with cancer weigh their options and learn how to take a holistic approach to cancer as an illness to be lived with, rather than an enemy to be attacked.

We had both started our quest for spiritual learning at the same time. We became certified in different energy medicine modalities and often discussed life after death and what it's like to die well and on one's own terms.

As for my father, he had always envisioned dying peacefully in his sleep, in a beautiful place surrounded by nature. Unfortunately, following a massive stroke, he died in an ICU with tubes hanging out of his head, in a lot of pain, and a potent dose of morphine running through his veins.

After his death, I became determined to find out more about the wishes of the dying and how to ensure that they are met. After all, as a hospice nurse, I sat beside many deathbeds - holding patients' hands, comforting their families, witnessing arguments over who gets grandma's rings or how their loved one should be buried. Even if their loved one's wishes were outlined prior to their last days, I saw families tear up advanced directives, revoke hospice documents, and return their loved one to the hospital against their expressed desire.

But I also sat beside those who held vigil, lit candles, told stories, and were truly present with their loved ones in their last days.

I learned what fear, grief, and unresolved emotions could do to prevent anyone from having a "good death," whether for their loved ones or themselves. It became apparent that if we hold life as a sacred event, then death should also be held as sacred. As we have heard many times, no one is getting out of here alive. Yet we kick and scream and hold on to the edge of a cliff all our lives, fearing the end and how it may manifest. In doing so, we forget to live a sacred life and lose the opportunity to have a sacred death.

But I hadn't fathomed that my little sister would teach me the biggest lesson on how to live and die on one's own terms.

Until my father's death, my sister had been living with cancer as a chronic illness, as she called it. She researched many alternative and complementary therapies and tried each as they were presented to her. Unfortunately, she could not find a doctor who would allow her to be a part of the decision-making process regarding her treatment until her disease had advanced. Yet, she was able to carry on and be there for my mother after my dad passed, as well as be a rock for everyone else in the family. She was convinced at times that she would beat cancer, and at times, she felt like she had no will to live.

Meanwhile, I had advanced my skills in energy medicine, indigenous studies, and other philosophies on death and dying. I saw that it was a gift and honor to be present with the dying and with the sacredness of the process. There is as much sacredness in bringing a baby into this world as there is in being present when one transitions from this world into the unseen.

The process of grief was front and center for all of us after the loss of our father. I dove into learning about coping with grief so I could help others someday, as my sister was trying to do with her cancer diary. My grieving became more complex as the anticipatory grief of losing my sister took over.

Nassim struggled with the fact that her wishes for how she wanted to make this journey were not accepted by the rest of her family and friends. Everyone around her had an opinion on how she should approach her illness. You name it, she was given it. In some ways, that can be a blessing. But when it conflicts with what you feel is right for you, it can create an internal battle that is hard to overcome if you lose your inner compass.

Witnessing this battle within my sister and within the family was hard.

She insisted that if she received chemo or the extensive surgery they had laid out for her, she would die right then and there. Personal beliefs play a huge role in how people go through any challenge in life. I have seen people beat advanced cancer through their belief system or succumb to it at an early stage.

As an empath, I could feel all sides of the situation: the grief and helplessness she felt and my own thoughts, impressions, and grief on top of that. All while trying to be objective as a nurse and advocate for my sister.

Nassim and I were not very close growing up. Years before her diagnosis, when we attended a self-improvement seminar that involved telling each other our true feelings about each other, she looked at me and said: "I hated you growing up. I am not sure why, but I always felt you were spoiled and privileged in our home." This made my tears start to roll, as I had no idea that my sister hated my guts that much. I had always considered her my rock, someone I would call a few times a day to run ideas by. I can still feel the pain in my gut hearing those words. But over time and more dialogue, we chose to forgive each other and move on.

Fast forward to 2012, the last year of her battle with cancer. Back surgery following a car accident had revealed that her cancer had metastasized to the bone, and there was less hope for beating the disease. However, she came through the surgery and shared with me that she felt she'd had a near-death experience under anesthesia. She told me: "I know you are the only person that can feel where I am coming from and can help me get through this, wherever it leads." Now my tears rolled for a different reason. She had chosen me to walk with her on the last stretch of her path. It was an honor and a privilege, though one that came with its own associated pain and sorrow. Yet, that truth is something I carry with me to this day, one I pull out of my emotional tool bag when I need to remember the privilege of being present with my patients and clients during their final passage.

The sense that her near-death experience had brought about remission did not leave my sister as she started to improve greatly during the weeks following her spinal surgery. She believed she was on the mend, and she was. We watched the Fourth of July fireworks from her hospital room window as we talked about the future and how she would share the knowledge and lessons from her spar with life and death. At times she would talk non-stop as if she were running out of time (some of this was a reaction to her medications), and at times she was very reflective. She imparted her wisdom and her challenges through times of sadness, depression, and joy. Yes, JOY. We laughed a lot, watching silly movies we both liked and at some of our happier memories of childhood.

During that year, I lived an hour and a half from my family and had a full-time job. I would leave after work to go to my sister's home two to three times a week and most weekends to help with whatever I could. The hardest days were when I went with her to give away her clothes to charity, divide up her jewelry for her sisters and nieces, arrange her own cremation, and close her bank account. I remember the woman at the bank looking at my sister's anorexic figure in disbelief when asking her why she was closing her account. The teller's face went pale when my sister replied, "I am dying!" I was shaking inside from grief and holding back the tears. Yet, I was also admiring her resolve in how she wanted her death done. She did not want to leave anything for others to do. My beautiful sister did not want to burden anyone and wanted her wishes to be followed at the same time.

It is ironic that she was the executor of my will, the guardian of my child, and she happened to be the one leaving. It shows that we can never really plan anything.

On some days toward the end, I don't know how she kept her balance as she was a mere shell of her former self after severe weight loss. Yet, she kept going, running errands for my mom and setting my mom's finances straight for when she would no longer be there to do so—spending quality time with everyone as much as possible when she felt up to it. Every evening when her pain would get too much to bear, she would call and say, "It's the witching hour. Please do some healing work to help my pain." Then I would start to cry myself. Some nights our family and friends got on the phone and said collective prayers, sending her love.

Each of us hid our pain inside so we would not add to her burden. This pain grew like a cancer itself and twisted around our guts and our hearts in unimaginable ways. We could not even imagine that this beautiful butterfly who was a source of mischief as a child and a rock for everyone to lean on as an adult would be leaving our plane of reality.

By October of 2012, all that spark was gone. The cancer had come back with a vengeance. I kept asking her, "What happened?" All she would say was that fear and doubt had entered her. She was giving into doubts that maybe she should have listened to the doctors and other people and chosen a different course. At the same time, she said, "I am tired of being told what to do, and I am tired of being here and in all this pain." The following months were excruciating for her and all of us in her circle.

In early July of 2013, she decided to admit herself to the hospital's inpatient hospice unit. They told her she could only be there for two weeks per Medicare rules. In other words, if she didn't die in two weeks, she would be discharged. My sister smirked and said, "You don't have to worry. I won't be here that long!"

During those two last weeks, she called friends whom she hadn't seen for a while, bravely gave them the rundown, and said her goodbyes. Some flew in from long distances or drove in and said goodbye in person. She made a lot of "completions," as she called them, and her spirit seemed lighter with each visit or conversation.

Three days before she took flight from this world, I helped her to the bathroom. She could barely hold her weight but insisted on dragging her pole with her pain meds hanging into the bathroom. She stopped for a second and said, "I can't believe I'm actually dying! I was just figuring out this week what life is about."

As she fell into her last slumber and her organs started to shut down, we sat vigil in her room, playing her favorite songs continuously on a computer. She would gently bob her head to the music even though she was fading away. I stayed in her room as everyone went home to rest and come back the next day. I kept the music going, Pink Martini, her favorite band. I can't even describe how my night was as I kept listening to the music and to her labored breathing—trying to remember all the words she imparted to me during her last months. In the morning, I was restarting the playlist when I noticed there was no sound. She had stopped breathing. My angel sister had the most beautiful smile on her face.

To this day, whenever I am somewhere and Pink Martini songs come on, I know she is watching and bobbing her head.

THE TOOL

As I mentioned, as a hospice nurse, I have been present by many deathbeds and witnessed many dynamics. However, until it is your own grief, you may not realize how the effects of it ripple through your life for years to come. The death of my father left a huge hole in our lives. My sister's death made that a crater! My mother, an amazingly resilient woman, went into deep despair and decided she did not want to live to see my sister's first anniversary. Circumstances came up that made her wish come true. She checked herself into hospice the following July and died two weeks before my sister's anniversary. She, too, died on her own terms.

Grief and loss are part of our daily lives regardless of our perception. Losing a loved one, divorce, moving, loss of a job, bankruptcy, break-up, the violence and other news happening on the world stage, all these changes are a part of our daily existence. How we accept and deal with them will help us stay rooted in fear, or enable us to move through and LIVE.

So to deal with my grief, I dove in to every article I could find, every book, and every seminar. I was a diehard fan of Elizabeth Kubler-Ross since nursing school. She really understood the needs of the dying and the stages of grief that follow. I took courses with David Kessler and Frank Ostaseski. I highly recommend their work. This is a summary of what I put into practice for myself and in my workshops on Grief and Loss:

- Realize that death is a given. None of us can escape it, at least not in the current reality. We can fear it and risk losing precious moments in our lives or LIVE FULLY despite the fact we will die someday. None of us know when that moment is.

  So every morning, wake up and ask yourself: "what would I do if today was my last day?"

- Science suggests that grief changes our brain chemistry in a similar way that repeated stress does. Science also indicates that the damage can be reversed if we can process the grief and train our brain and outlook.

  When your emotions rise, instead of pushing them down, feel them as if you are riding on an ocean wave. The wave comes up, then subsides until the next wave. If the emotion is anger, feel it, scream out loud, punch a pillow, go for a walk, yell at the universe. You get the picture.

- Don't compare your grief to others. Everyone grieves according to how their mind and body can process it and as long as it takes.

  Teach those around you who are trying to help how they can be helpful to you. They really don't know! Sometimes I would ask a friend just to sit with me and not say anything.

- BREATHE! *Deep belly breathe. Inhale for a count of four, pause for four, exhale for four and pause for four. You can change the count to fit your comfort level. This resets your vagus nerve and stress response.*

- Spend time in nature. *It is invaluable the peace it brings.*

- Keep a journal of your grief. Daily if possible. *Write affirmations in it and read them at times of heightened emotions.*

- Do whatever brings Joy. LAUGH. *This is a choice!*
- Light a candle and talk to your departed loved one. *Feel them around you.*
- Make your wishes known to your circle and make advanced directives. *Don't wait.*

Shabnam Hashemi, BSN, RN, comes with over 30 years of experience in healthcare. She has a hybrid background in laboratory science, public health, nursing, and complementary medicine. She currently works as a hospice nurse.

Her goal is to help others navigate through grief and trauma as well as release physical pain, which often has roots in emotional trauma. She utilizes her own life experiences, studies, and the gift of empathy to guide clients through their healing journey. Her expertise extends to helping families going through a death of a loved one and coping with loss. Shabnam is a Reiki Master/Teacher level practitioner and practices Clinical Aromatherapy, Craniosacral therapy, Shamanic Healing, and Tong Ren.

Recently developed workshops include:

- Living with Grief and Loss – A multifaceted Journey (presented at Scripps Health Care and Sharps Memorial in San Diego, CA)
- Walking your talk-Emerging from Burnout into Resilience through Self-care
- Ancient tools for modern times- Shamanic tools for everyday living
- Navigating Fear

You can find out more about her from her website: www.shabnamhashemi.com or contact her via email at: info@shabnamhashemi.com

CHAPTER 3

BREATH

THE VERY FIRST AND LAST ACT OF YOUR LIFE

Dr. Krupa Vora-Knarr, Pharm. D

MY STORY

"You are doing so good; keep up the pace; you are almost there. Keep going! Hooray, way to go." The crowds thunderous cheers, at times deafening, was filled with joy as I ran with other runners nearing the boardwalk of Virginia Beach. The first 11 miles felt euphoric, with a steady speed and breathing; nothing hurt; it felt freeing. The cool weather helped to keep my body temperature down. Then the aching sensations began; I started being anxious, my breathing became heavy, and I was almost gasping for air. My legs felt wooden and I began to feel the cracks and bumps on the pavement. Strong emotions started coming over me; *I can't do this anymore, I can't breathe; why did I decide to run a half marathon? My legs feel so heavy; with every step forward, it feels like I am moving a mountain.* My heart was racing, pounding as if it was going to break out of my rib cage. I was exhausted. I was at the 11.5-mile mark and just couldn't go any further. I was out of breath and my knees were giving up.

"Here, hold on to this; we are almost there; we're going to cross the finish line." Seeing me struggle to move, my best friend slowed down and handed me one end of her white hand towel; a lifeline for me to crawl myself out of a deep dark hole. The hard and inconsistent breathing soon became calmer. She pulled me forward for a mile until I could gather my strength, breathe naturally, gain my balance, and muster enough power to continue independently. I am and will be forever grateful to her for signing me up for this race to help me get out of my rock bottom. I never owned a good pair of running shoes, but running was just the beginning of my journey from complicated grief. It started out as a distraction from all my pain and trauma, a way to numb myself and exhaust my body and mind to the point I didn't have to feel anything. More importantly, running helped me gain weight, breathe better, and helped me release my emotions.

My world changed seven months prior to that half-marathon when I lost my papa to a short battle of Pulmonary Fibrosis. He raised us with a mantra that girls can do everything boys can. He was our pillar, a true hero, our avenger who motivated, encouraged, and guided us to live a heart-centered, purposeful life. He prepared us to be independent at a very young age, just in case something happened to him. I was my papa's little girl. I still remember the day, how excited and proud he felt when I finished my Doctorate in Pharmacy. Not to mention the moment when he found out I would be supporting my spouse as he went to pursue his medical schooling in the Caribbean. My papa knew the importance of sacrifice and did not question how that would impact my marriage.

Four months before he died, I moved back home from Florida (with my parents) due to a job relocation. It was during this time that he developed a cough that kept getting worse. Initial testing yielded nothing before I took him to a cardiologist to run a CT scan. The lower left lobe of his lung had a very distinctive honeycomb structure pattern, which suggested Pulmonary Fibrosis. Knowing this disease had no cure, with a maximum of seven years life expectancy, I was devastated. We were ready to turn the world upside down to find something or someone who could help him. With the help of a friend, we could get an appointment with a top-ranked pulmonologist at Johns Hopkins Medical Center. However, his breathing was deteriorating quickly, and he eventually needed a portable oxygen concentrator to stay active during the day. My sister and I took care of my dad and younger brother, who was recovering from a fall that left him bed-ridden for almost six months. My mom, papa, brother, and I temporarily moved in with my sister and her family to make it easy for us. And yes, you guessed it correctly, the family dynamics took their toll on us. I mainly took care of my papa's weekly doctor visits, and my sister took care of my brother's doctor visits.

One cold Friday evening, my papa was too tired to walk upstairs to sleep and decided to lay down on the couch. I pulled out a cozy warm blanket and tucked him in, wishing him good night. He didn't need to use the loud oxygen machine at night, so I turned it off and decided to sleep across from him on a big sofa chair. I mumbled, "Papa, please wake me up if you need anything," and dozed off. A loud thud woke me up. At first, I thought I was dreaming but jumped out of the chair to check on him. He was not on the couch. I ran around the corner and saw him on the floor, sitting against the wall. Our eyes locked; he was still conscious and didn't want me to make a fuss. I screamed for my brother-in-law to call an ambulance and frantically woke everyone else in the house.

By the time I got to the ER, Papa was surrounded by a team of nurses and doctors, hooking him up with an IV, EKG, and oxygen mask. He was irritated and confused with the chaos in the room and was uncomfortable with the oxygen mask on. He kept on removing it to breathe. I stood at the foot of his bed, gesturing him to look and follow me, raising my right hand up to breathe in and down to cue him to breathe out. This was an exercise we practiced several times after he was prescribed the portable oxygen machine. I matched my breath with his shallow breathing, in and out, and he finally relaxed so the nurses could draw his blood and assess him. A few hours later, the results were in. He was diagnosed with pneumonia, and his blood pressure and oxygen levels were too low. He was immediately moved to ICU. When he was settled in his bed, he looked outside the window and asked, "Did it snow more than an inch?" Papa was feeling better and was ready to talk to everyone who entered the room. A few different doctors came in to check him, and one of them stayed a little longer to ask about his background and work, trying to find the cause of his lung disease. Then the doctor slowly started talking about advance directives—to prepare him and the family. My papa pointed his finger at me, implying, "my kids know my wishes." The last few weeks, he went through all his photo albums and shared his life stories and experiences. He told us, "I have a wonderful family, beautiful grandkids, and loving friends. I have had a happy life. If it is my time to go, I am okay."

I stepped away for a few minutes, and as I approached the room, I saw a doctor controlling my papa's airflow with a manual resuscitator bag. Things didn't look good. Soon his vitals began to drop, and he was sedated and intubated. I stood there crying, praying, and begging for his lungs just to breathe. The doctor came out, "He is currently stable on the ventilator, but it's time to call the rest of his family." His lungs were damaged and at 23% capacity. We had family and friends, local and out of state, all gathered around him and quietly praying by his bedside in few hours. I finally signed a "Do Not Resuscitate" form and joined the rest of the family in that decision. We all said our goodbyes, but we could still hear his labored breath along with the ventilator. A week prior, my best friend mentioned, "Your dad may not want to leave you guys, so be prepared to say it's okay to go." We told him that we loved him and said our goodbye hoping he was listening. We still heard his heartbeat through the EKG monitor above our head. "Papa, we will take care of each other, love each other, and always be there for each other; please don't worry about us; we love you. It's okay to leave us." As soon as I said that, the EKG monitor showed a flat line.

On January 31st, 2010, my papa passed away. I was in disbelief, that sinking feeling; *How am I going to go on without him?* He was my backbone, my captain. He was one person I turned to for advice, and I knew he was always there to guide and support me. *How do I deal with this grief?* Just as we were trying to come to terms with our loss, I got hit by another crisis. It was a late-night call that shook my world, sending me to a full-blown panic attack. "I am having an affair." My now ex-husband unapologetically shared this over the phone. This is where my grief got a little complicated. I was numb for the rest of the night and fell asleep sobbing without sharing it with any of my family. The sun peeked through my window, and for a moment, I thought: *was that a dream? Did this really happen?* That feeling of numbness took over my body again. I checked my phone and saw the call. Reality hit me: *How am I going to share this with my immediate family at a time when they are already hurting?* I was irritated, angry, and my mind ran at lightning speed. All I wanted to do was smash every picture frame until the glass pieces covered the floor.

Looking back, that was the breaking point of my life. I lost weight and started experiencing frequent panic attacks. I felt like something was crawling under my skin for days and just couldn't shake it off. One night, after a twelve-hour shift, I was getting ready to come home, sitting in the parking lot. I took a deep breath and closed my eyes. I visualized holding a knife in one hand to the wrist of the other. I imagined slitting my wrist and blood gushing everywhere. But it wasn't just blood that was leaving my body. Black creepy crawlies were coming out as well. Then I opened my eyes and took another deep breath, and let out the biggest sigh. I felt at peace. That was the turning point, a turning point from rock bottom. I knew I needed to change and seek alternate means to heal myself. This is when my journey to heal from the inside began.

THE TOOL

Breath is the essence of life. As soon as we are born, we take our first breath, and we continue breathing until we take our last one. This is a task our body performs naturally, unconsciously, and involuntarily. Our natural breathing varies depending on our physical, mental, and emotional conditions. When these conditions are compromised, the breath is shallow and labored, indicating our sympathetic nervous system is activated (fight-flight-freeze response). On the other hand, deep and slow breaths stimulate our parasympathetic nervous system response and ease us into a "calm, rest, and digest" state. This is why it's essential we learn to breathe consciously.

I grew up watching my parents practice pranayama every morning, followed by asanas. Pranayama is the management of prana, or life force energy, an ancient practice of controlling your breath. You control the timing, duration, and frequency of every incoming and outgoing breath, along with a pause or hold. Holding your breath gives your body enough time to exchange oxygen to cells and expel carbon dioxide. I realized that we could learn to work with our own breath to lower anxiety and depression, energize the body, reduce stress, help us sleep, and even balance our hyperactive mind. I have compiled a list of my favorite techniques I have learned from my teachers.

Before you start, take a moment to check in with yourself. Sit comfortably with your back straight and without judgment, observe how each inhalation and exhalation feels. What sensations are you experiencing, and which physical movements occur? Now fully breathe in and out. This anchors your focus to the present moment so you can receive the full benefits.

SAMVRITTI SQUARE AND SOOTHING BREATH FOR STRESS AND ANXIETY

1. Samvritti Square breathing or box breathing is very simple to learn and practice anywhere. I use it at work and teach my patients this when they pick up their anxiety pills. I trace a box shape with my finger on my palm while counting my breath:

   • Breathe in for a count of 4.

   • Hold for a count of 4.

   • Breathe out for a count of 4.

   • Hold for a count of 4.

2. A soothing breath acts as a natural tranquilizer for the nervous system. This technique has helped me breathe better during my panic attacks and migraines as well. I use it while driving, during stressful situations, and for sleep. At first, it's best to perform the exercise seated with your back straight. Once you become more familiar with the breathing exercise, you can perform it while lying in bed:

   • Breathe in for a count of 4

   • Hold for a count of 4

   • Breathe out for a count of 6

   • Hold out for a count of 2

BENEFITS

Continue this breathing pattern for a minute or two. It slows your heart rate, blood pressure lowers, stress melts away, and muscles begin to relax.

UJJAYI PRANAYAMA FOR CALMING AND CENTERING

Also known as "victorious or ocean breath." I combine this technique with the soothing breath count for deeper relaxation.

- Start by breathing through your mouth, making a quiet 'ha' sound as you exhale.
- Then close your mouth, keep this sound going as you breathe in and out through the nose.
- While you are breathing through your nose, you slightly constrict the back of the throat, so your voice makes a quiet sound, almost like light snoring.
- Keep your inhalations and exhalations equal in durations.

BENEFITS

It improves your concentration and releases tension throughout the body. It regulates heating and cooling of the body, warming the core from the inside. You can use it anytime, anywhere. Breathing like this will help you fall asleep at night and keep your mind in the present.

ANULOM VILOM - ALTERNATE NOSTRIL BREATHING TO SETTLE A BUSY MIND

Performed generally in the morning on an empty stomach, or two to three hours after a meal. This technique is safe for most healthy adults. It's a good idea to start with just a minute or two and slowly increase as your confidence grows. I have sometimes visualized this technique to help me settle my mind.

Start with your hands resting on your knees with palms facing up.

- Place the tip of the index finger and middle finger of the right hand in between the eyebrows with the ring finger and pinky finger on the left nostril and the thumb on the right nostril.

- On an exhalation, close the right nostril with your thumb and breathe out through the left nostril.

- Breathe in through the left nostril and then close with the ring finger.

- Release the thumb on the right nostril and breathe out through the right nostril.

- Inhale through the right nostril, close with the thumb, release the ring finger from the left side and exhale through the left nostril.

- This is one round of Anulom Vilom; practice this breathing for 1-5 minutes.

BENEFITS

Alternate nostril breathing activates the parasympathetic nervous system, lowers blood pressure, increases the endurance of the respiratory system, and balances the left and right hemispheres of the brain.

KAPALBHATI – BREATH OF FIRE FOR DIGESTION AND DETOXIFICATION

Performed generally in the morning on an empty stomach, or two to three hours after a meal.

- Inhale deeply through both nostrils, expand the chest.

- Start exhaling with force while squeezing in the stomach.

- Expel the breath with forceful contractions of the abdominal muscles and relax.

- Do not strain.

- Continue active/forceful exhalation and passive inhalation.

- Complete 30 rapid breaths, then take a deep breath and exhale slowly.

- This is one round of Kapalbhati.

- Each round shall be followed by deep breathing.

Number of rounds: Beginners can practice up to three rounds of 20 breaths each. The count and rounds can be increased gradually over a period of time.

BENEFITS

It balances and strengthens the nervous system as well as tones the digestive system. It is useful in treating cold, rhinitis, sinusitis, asthma, and bronchial infections. It rejuvenates the whole body and keeps the face young and vibrant.

Caution:

- Please avoid this practice in case of cardiac conditions, dizziness, high blood pressure, pregnancy, vertigo, chronic bleeding in the nose, epilepsy, migraine, stroke, hernia, and gastric ulcers.

CONCLUSION

In the last five years, I have made a conscious effort to learn yoga. Yoga is more than just moving your body in different poses. Breathwork is more integral because conscious breathing creates that deep mind-body spiritual connection that makes yoga so beneficial for calming the mind and understanding one's self. My instructor used to say: "It is only when your awareness and breath are yoked together that you start to be able to experience your body through your breath, instead of through the thinking and judging part of your brain." My wish for you is to be in awareness with your breath in every moment. All the rises and drops, the racing and slowing, the tethered, the stuck, the tight and gasping. Give yourself permission to feel the stillness, peace, and joy in the holds between the inhales and exhales. Accept them all and release that what is keeping you stuck. Flow with the rhythm of your breath. Let your every breath on this beautiful planet count.

Dr. Krupa Vora-Knarr is a Certified Radiant Child Yoga Instructor, Reiki practitioner (level 1 and 2), and Doctor of Pharmacy. Krupa has been working as a Pharmacist for over 18 years and enjoys counseling her patients about medications, mindful breathing, yoga, and ayurvedic diet. She began practicing yoga and breathwork at a very young age growing up in India. Krupa is passionate about introducing yoga and mindful breathing to children at an early age as it provides tools for practicing compassion, mindfulness, generosity, focus, confidence, strength, and flexibility. Her typical class leads you through a gentle warm-up and a combination of storytelling/adventure-themed creative movements. This is followed by a heat-building sequence, a cool down to recharge relaxation, and finally meditation. During relaxation, Krupa uses a healing hand technique that she learned in Reiki to center and further relax young yogis and yoginis. She has been teaching children yoga with Create Calm since 2019 and is a volunteer yoga teacher at her son's Sunday school. She is currently studying in a 200-hour yoga teacher training course.

To learn more, please visit her website: Inspiredbreathyoga.com

or email her: Inspiredbreathyoga@gmail.com.

www.instagram.com/mikrulove

CHAPTER 4

MIDWIFING MIRACLES AND MESSENGERS OF LOVE

CREATING A LIVING ALTAR TO HONOR AND CONNECT WITH YOUR LOVED ONES

Reverend Stephanie Urbina Jones, "Shaman Heart,"
Toltec Transformational Teacher, Preacher,
#1 Billboard Songwriter

MY STORY

"I can't remember how many million tears I've cried

Nights that I have stayed awake asking God why

This world is sometimes filled with so much pain and sorrow

Wondering if the sun would ever shine on my tomorrow"

I was born into a bicultural home in the heart of San Antonio, Texas. My first memories were ones of friends and family, backyard barbecues, tamales, country music, mariachis, and the safety of my abuelito's arms. He was my person. I was his Patootie. I'd almost always be perched beside him on my rooster stool he bought me, watching Mexican wrestling or Sabado Gigante while my grandmother made *pollo con arroz* and my favorite red enchiladas. Each day he would take my little hand and walk me down to the corner pharmacy for chocolate ice cream, and on special days I'd cuddle up to him in his Pontiac and ride down to Rays Drive-In where he'd order chalupas, a Pearl beer, and a Big Red for me. We'd sit there for hours, dropping quarters in the jukebox listening to Hank Williams, Patsy Cline, Ray Price, and Boleros from Mexico. He adored me like no one did or ever would. While things were crazy in my young parents' home, they were joy-filled and calm at my abuelo's house at 115 North Cibolo. There, friends and family came and went, the radio from the border blared, and there was always a pot of beans on the stove. I had no idea then that things were about to change. Soon my grandpa went from three-piece suits and shined up shoes to striped pajamas and slippers. First, he lost his toe, then his foot, and then they amputated his leg up to his hip. All I knew was that I was so grateful to spend more time with my grandpa. I don't remember the day he died, but I know that life went from technicolor to black and white overnight. Soon I was standing in the doorway of a big room with a wooden box at the front. I had no idea what I was walking into. I was so happy to see my tias, tios, family, neighbors, and loved ones. At some point, I, too, made my way up to the box at the front of the room. I stood on the steps and peeked in. There in front of me was my ghost-white grandpa. I let out a curdling scream that came from deep inside of me, calling for him to "come back!" I wanted to climb in that box and go with him wherever he had gone. I loved him so much. He was my safe place, the one who got me and kept the family and my parents, who were now divorced, calm. I was inconsolable. At four years old, as they laid him in the grave, a part of me died and went with him. I was frozen in time, and it would take many years for that little girl to find her way back to life.

"Sometimes sadness seems like an old friend

Someone who really knows just how hard it's been

Tears come to me and give dignity to the secrets in my soul

Till I am all cried out and ready to let go"

Time marched on from my teens to my twenties, and I gratefully discovered music to keep me grounded and connected to life. I had a suitcase record player, and it reached into my closet where I could almost close the door of my little womb of a room. Crouched in my closet, I would play my album, *Tapestry*. It was a gift from my dad, who I rarely got to see, and it meant the world to me. There, I'd escape into the arms of my favorite song, rocking myself to *You've Got a Friend*, over and over again. After college, I followed my heart to Nashville, where I became a staff writer for Sony ATV Tree Music. It was an amazing way to tell my truth, purge my pain, and carve out my soul in song while trying to make sense of this desperate longing still living inside me. While I did not consciously understand the impact of my grandpa's passing back then, it haunted me every day. I had become a master at seeking relief in all sorts of ways from that old emotional pain and other trauma seared into my body. During this same time, I discovered and became obsessed with the book, *The Wheel of Life, A Memoir of Living and Dying* by Dr. Elisabeth Kubler-Ross. I was particularly struck by her journey to the Maideneck Concentration Camps in Poland after WWII and her recollection of visiting the children's barracks. There she was surprised and amazed to find hundreds of butterflies carved into the walls with pebbles and their fingernails. She wondered why they were there and what they meant. Over years of working with terminally ill patients, she understood that these carvings were messengers from the children knowing that soon they would die and be out of this hellish place. Soon they would leave their bodies like cocoons and emerge as butterflies. It was a message for generations to come and one for me as well. The book gave me great hope and the beginning of an understanding that would someday transform my life and lead me to my life's work. Since my grandfather died, I, too, wanted to escape this life and find my way out of my cocoon. I kept on writing.

"Like a butterfly needs to find its way out of a cocoon

In this life we all have things we've got to struggle through

From the darkness we are led to the light of truth

Where sacred wounds are healed and we are Born from the Blues"

It was no coincidence that within that same year, my dad would provide another cosmic breadcrumb on my life's journey. One day as we walked, he talked about his days in Vietnam as a foreign observer with the 101st Airborne. He knew any day could be his last. He carried a little picture of me as a prayer to keep him grounded and alive. He often said the horrors of war made them all believers and that there were no atheists in fox holes. He said that in the jungle, you become acutely aware with sharpened instincts to see into and beyond this world. He shared that often, just before a soldier died, he would see his spirit leave his body. It was almost as if the grace of God would take him before the pain of dying. He said that sometimes before a battle, he would see fields of spirits ascending from this world to the next. This conversation with my dad that summer rocked and scared me, but only because I knew it was true. Not too long down the road, I, too, would be ripening my tools and midwifing a miracle that would change the course of my life and bring me the peace I was longing for. I was 33, and another turn of the wheel was just around the corner.

"Like a mother gives birth to a baby boy or girl

Like a father searching to find his place in this world

Like a singer whose sorrow finally finds a song to sing

Like a dying man who understands that his soul has wings"

Within a few months, I got a call from my grandma, Virginia. I picked up the phone, and the first words out of her mouth were, "Mija, I'm dying." She'd been talking about it for years, but I knew at that moment that this was it. Some part of me I never knew before locked and loaded with a presence I can still feel in my body today. I flew to be by her side. There I sat in holy communion between life and death with Señora Jones, my beloved feisty, spicy, and sometimes mean little Mexican grandmother. We laughed, cried, reminisced, and put many things to rest, including the outfit and red lipstick she wanted to be buried in. Suddenly her attention would be drawn somewhere above her, and she'd begin a full-blown conversation with my grandfather, her sister, Armida, my great grandfather, Manuel, or her mother, Cerrita, on the other side. She was walking between the worlds.

Days turned to a week, and then in one transcendent moment, she took my hand, looked at and through me, and said, "Mija, you will be a *mensajera*. You will be a voice for our people, sharing our beautiful Mexican culture with the world." She giggled and said, "You will be making country music with chili peppers." It was obviously a transmission from heaven, but I was not ready for it. I rebutted, saying, "Grandma, I can't do it. I am too insecure, and I don't even speak Spanish." She looked at me and, with calm resolve, said, "Mija, you will." I can't remember what day it was because time stood still. All I know is that the doctor said I could go home because it would be a few days before she passed. I knew differently. I knew she was going to be passing within the next few hours. I called my dad and tio, Rudy, and we held a prayer vigil. The room was pregnant with peace and an indescribable full, potent, condensed love. It was the most holy experience of my life besides having my own daughter Zeta. I can't remember exactly when it was, but I know that I knew when it was time. I called my dad and tio, and we gathered around her. She was no longer conscious to talk, but she was still present in her body and at peace. Her skin was translucent, and her breathing became labored, in and out, in and out. It really was like childbirth; I could feel her spirit as it began to make its way to the point of releasing and rebirthing. "In and out," I said to my dad, "here we go." She took one more deep breath, and I swear I saw her spirit fly, a faint white wisp out of the top of her head. At the very same moment that she slipped out of her body and shed her skin, I felt this jubilation in my body and spirit as her soul was freed. It was so surreal to be so connected with her and to feel so happy, almost giddy, in that moment. I remember thinking, *this is so strange,* as I took my finger and poked her body. She was no longer there; it was a carcass; she was gone. In that moment, there were no tears, only holy awe. I was the witness to the sacred death and rebirth of my grandmother from this world to the next.

While I was raised in Catholic and Methodist religions, I did not have an experience of God or something beyond me until this. I felt the great mystery and knew beyond a shadow of a doubt that there was life beyond this one. It filled me with wonder and excitement to be alive. In the days and years to come, the cosmic breadcrumbs began to reveal a reverent understanding of the twists and turns that led me here, but before then, the dam broke, and years of deep, unexpressed grief came in waves. In those broken open moments, that little girl who was frozen in time long ago slowly but surely found her way back. My grandmother's sacred passing helped me begin to honor and release the trauma I held in my body all those years before, and I came back to live with a fiery passion for life. I had dreams, seeds planted in my heart as a child, and with this thawing out of pain came the desire to live those dreams. From that day forward, I became as focused on living as I had been about dying. I began to dream and believe in miracles, empowered with the knowing that I was being guided. Red birds, butterflies, and/or sage advice from the grocery store bagger dropped in out of nowhere to reveal my next right step every time.

I soon found the courage and means to begin making records and stepping into and through my fear. One miracle after another unfolded since that time 20 years ago, and I am humbled to share that just as she had seen, I went on to record nine albums, traveled the world as a *mensajera* (messenger of love), celebrating our culture in song and making history with my "country music with chili peppers." I went on to purge my pain and found ways to not only transcend it but to turn it into my medicine, becoming a Toltec Transformational teacher. I now gratefully walk with others and hold sacred witness as they midwife the miracles in their own lives, turning their pain into purpose. At the core of every song, every show, every teaching, every moment is life, death, rebirth, and love.

From that day to now, I have been guided and supported and am blessed by this map of pain and transformation that has led me to share this message of hope all over the world. In all my travels, I carry and create little altars everywhere to work my prayers. I surrender to the great unknown and ask for wisdom and help. I place my faith and my heart on the altar, then meditate, pray, and pay attention, building the holy knowing and intuition that I first experienced when midwifing my grandmother so many moons ago. While I am human and will always deeply miss and mourn my loved ones, I am grateful to know that there is a divine force available just when I need it most.

Call it God, call it guides, call it angels; whatever you call it, we are not alone.

THE TOOL

CREATING AN ALTAR TO HONOR AND CONNECT WITH YOUR LOVED ONES

Choose a special place in your home where you can create a sacred ceremony and build your altar.

Start by gathering your favorite pictures and mementos that remind you of your loved ones. Find some music, either meditative or songs that remind you of your loved one, and create a song list. Find a piece of fabric, altar cloth, or some old lace, clothes that remind you of your loved one, to be the foundation of your altar, and a candle for the center. Close your eyes breathing deeply for five to ten minutes allowing your heart and mind to drop into the memories of your loved one. Keep a box of tissues close by. When you feel you've connected to their heart, open your eyes and light a candle in the center of your altar. Allow your heart and spirit to commune with your loved one. If you have questions about your life, ask in the silence of this ceremony. Grow your trust and faith and let this altar be your offering of love to honor their life but also to honor yours. Change pictures, change objects, light some sage or copal, and change it up. Keep open to how they will communicate with you. Keep a journal as a witness to the miracles. Put feet to your prayers and suspend disbelief. They want to help and guide you in your life. Work this altar as if it was a line of communication from this world to the next. Soon it will be, and you too will be in communion beyond the veil with those you love.

For more information on this tool, to see a collection of my many altars, large and small, and or experience a Journey to the Ancestors with our Toltec Sacred Journey Breathwork, join me on my resource page at https://www.freedomfolkandsoul.org/stephanie-urbina-jones-shaman-heart

Stephanie Urbina Jones

Singer, teacher, writer, sister, friend, mother, wife, and lover of life; Stephanie Urbina Jones brings her passion and experience in living a life of creative freedom to people all over the world. Jones has a passion for transformation and is a living example of not only dreaming but bringing those dreams to life.

Whether she is writing a song, producing a festival, performing, or leading journeys of transformation as co-founder of Freedom Folk and Soul, a Transformational Community of the Healing Arts, Stephanie is truly following her heart and chiseling out her soul. She sees herself as a kind of midwife, guiding folks on their journey of self-discovery, healing, and transformation, empowering those who seek to live a life of passion, purpose, and personal freedom.

Stephanie has spent over 25 years in pursuit of her personal freedom. She has studied, prayed, walked, talked, worked, and turned over stones in the road and in her heart to heal and create a life of humility, passion, and purpose. Having personally experienced the journey of continuous transformation, she is called to give back what she has been given and share her experience, strength, and hope with other souls on the path of wellness and higher consciousness.

A true "walker between the worlds," SUJ shares inspiration in music from her album "Shaman Heart," a transformational journey in song with audiences and fellow journeyers everywhere.

SUJ is a # 1 Billboard Country Music Songwriter traveling with her Honky Tonk Mariachis, sharing joy and her history-making "Country Music with Chili Peppers" all over the world.

www.freedomfolkandsoul.org

www.stephanieurbinajones.com

www.freedomfolkandsoul.org/stephanie-urbina-jones-shaman-heart

CHAPTER 5

PIERCE THE VEIL

CONNECT TO SPIRITS BEHIND
THE CURTAIN OF DEATH

Atlantis Wolf

"Everything you can imagine is real."

-Pablo Picasso

I did not always see spirit guides, power animals, and galactic dragons; my gifts were awakened before and after a death—my mother's death—in the time when the worlds of the physical body and spiritual body open to each other, the time of the last human experience, when the veil between worlds is so thin it's almost transparent.

MY STORY

"I can't taste the pie," my mom said, sitting across from me at the round, oak dining room table.

"It's apples, flour, and sugar. Not much to taste," I said, not looking up as I glanced through photos of her garden club trip to southern Italy.

"My taste has been going since I got back from the trip," she said, finishing the slice.

"Do you think it's related to your fall?" I said, still turning over the stack of smiling strangers, terraced gardens, and tables of food.

"I doubt it," she said. "That was the back of my head, not my tongue."

We both laughed the same laugh.

After four months, her taste did not come back, and her short-term memory faded into nothing. She went to several doctors and eventually with my dad to an assisted living center for patients with Alzheimer's. The presiding doctor of the center sat with us in his office.

"I've seen this before," the doctor said. "She'll be gone within nine months."

She lasted six. She was 58. Her mother was 78, living next door. I was 38, still married then, and living 30 minutes away. My kids were six and four.

My dad and his good insurance took her to doctors, specialists, neurosurgeons for scans, spinal fluid tests, cognition exams, and hospital observations. The best neurologist in the city read the results and talked to my dad, sitting next to my mom, who had lost her ability to speak and struggled with cognition.

"She has a virus in her spinal fluid that's now in her brain," the neurologist said. "We can't pinpoint the exact strain. It's depleting the oxygen supply. There's nothing I can do. I wouldn't recommend treating the cancer either. The virus is likely to act quickly."

"What cancer?" my dad said.

"I'm sorry," said the neurologist. "Looking at the hospital reports, the tests came back for cancer. I thought you knew."

As a family, we buried the memory of breast cancer five years ago when she finished treatment and was in remission. We never talked about it. In the spectrum of neurological tests and evaluations, one of the doctors had just ordered a test for cancer. My dad had not yet returned the call from the doctor's office. He had been traveling for business all week and my mom was at my house with me and my two kids. As the three of us walked without words from the office to the parking lot, my dad looked at me.

"Tell everyone she has cancer," he said. "The rest is too complicated."

My dad turned to a traveling faith healer that came to their church, a rife machine therapist thirty minutes into the country, and a Reiki practitioner who made house calls. I accompanied my mom for all the sessions, including the first time the Reiki practitioner came to her house.

I was in her bedroom, sitting cross-legged at the end of her bed. The smell of fresh white gardenias in a blue glass vase on her nightstand filled the air from her side of the bed. A picture of the four of us at our house in the Caribbean sat beside it. Her pink cashmere beret from England was there, too, to cover her thin hair at night when she was cold. Her favorite Maxfield Parrish print, Ecstasy, the one of the woman standing on a rocky outcrop at the ocean with her hands lifting her hair and the wind wrapping her white dress around her body, was on the wall as it had been my whole life. The four walls kept the voices of my dad and brother outside of them. She was laying on a massage table, eyes closed, and fidgeting her arms and legs while the Reiki practitioner stood at her head, hovering her hands over my mother's flannel-covered shoulders.

Here I am, Mom. I don't have any instructions. I hate watching you get smaller every day. I don't know what to do.

I closed my eyes, imagining a ball the size of a cantaloupe being formed between my open hands. The ball was blue, formed like a cloud that was condensing into a more solid form. With eyes still closed, I pulsed my hands together back and forth an inch or so, making it feel more and more solid. When I couldn't compress the energy more, when it felt firm, I sent it over towards my mom's body. *Here is a ball of strength, Mom. Take it and use it for what you need. I give you my strength.* The ball sank into her body like a setting sun at the horizon as I let the tears rise and fall.

The moment the ball was absorbed into her body, I smiled through a face of tears, satisfied I had done something more than sitting like a pile of laundry on her bed. I opened my eyes and saw the Archangel Gabriel in the left corner of the ceiling, looking at my mother. He had blonde curls, mint-green robes, 20-foot wide white wings outstretched, and was surrounded by clouds and blue sky as if he temporarily dissolved the structure of the house and I was seeing into celestial realms. Time dissolved, too. No breathing, no blinking, no cancer, as if I could observe this holy moment for an infinite amount of time.

CHAPTER 5 | 39

"Grab her ankles!" the Reiki practitioner said. "She's fussing around. Ground her."

I blinked and breathed, breaking the spell.

I walked to her feet, standing with my hands around her ankles and holding her heels in my palms. The Archangel Gabriel flew over my head. His wing feathers touched my shoulders, and I felt the hairs on the top of my head whisked forward. I saw the back of his enormous wings over my mother's body.

I forgot how big his wings are.

I blinked. He was gone.

The Reiki practitioner finished her session. The home health-care nurse came to help my mom to her bed. I kissed my mom goodbye. She was peaceful and still in her bed by the gardenias.

"Did you see anything?" my dad asked the Reiki practitioner when she stepped outside the room. "You know she sees things," he said to me.

I said nothing.

"No," said the practitioner. "Nothing definitive. A few fuzzy shapes."

A month after seeing Gabriel, I woke, alone in bed, in the quietest, darkest hour of sleep, to see a ball of pulsing, white light about five feet in diameter all around me, like being in the center of a pollinated, electric dandelion in a gentle breeze. I looked to the pillow next to me to see a smaller ball of light.

"Oh, hi Mom!" I said.

"I'm giving you my power," she said.

"Okay," I said, rolling back to sleep.

Three days later, I was in her bedroom holding her hand when she opened her eyes and looked over my right shoulder. I saw the celestial realms in her eyes as she exhaled her last breath.

"She's looking right at you!" my dad said from the other side of her bed.

No, I thought. *She's not looking at me, but I know what she's seeing.*

An unexplainable, sudden, and effervescent jubilation filled me. I felt like my body was ballooning with golden sparkles and white light. I left to go home within minutes. My mother's voice was in my head, talking without a pause for 40 minutes as I drove home about all the events since she lost her voice. She had something to say about my dad, the home health aide, her mother, and my kids. We talked to each other the way we always talked, with quick-paced joy and naked sharing. We had no secrets from each other, especially now.

"I always told you we are like one soul in two bodies," she said. "Now, we can share this body."

"That's going to be an adjustment for me, Mom," I said. "Like moving an elephant into your apartment. You're taking up a lot of room in here!"

We both laughed the same laugh.

When I arrived at my house and stepped out of my car, I said, "You know, Mom, maybe this isn't the way it's supposed to be. If you want to go…"

With a whoosh feeling up and out of my right side, she left my body and ascended into a blue sky. I was alone, empty. Motherless.

After her death, I felt like an invisible hand dropped me into a well of black water with stone walls too high to climb, where no light could reach me. My only goal was to survive and keep my head above the numbing waters. Every time I thought of my mom, my throat filled with tears, and I became paralyzed with the loss of my second soul. I cried alone, only alone. So I stopped thinking about her and focused on getting out of bed every day, feeding my kids before and after they went to school, and sitting in a beige cubicle in a beige building with beige people.

I didn't write or reach out to friends or look in the mirror. After months, I wrote one line in my journal: *Scratched, patched, bruised, and bleeding.*

The darkness found me. I felt as if the lifetime of joy sharing my mother's company was lived in credit, and now with her death, a price was extracted all at once: an equal amount of grief. I lived in the well of black waters for more than a year until the struggle drained me, and I sank below the surface, baptized in death, surrendered to never feeling her love again.

Dear God, I'm not going to make it. I'm not going to live another day. Please help me. Tell me where you need me, and I'll bloom. Tell me tonight while I sleep. Put me where you need me. I'll do anything you ask. I need something that will provide for my children and myself. I need this house. Whatever you tell me, I'll do it. I make a promise to you now. Save me. Find me.

I fell into a windowless, silent stretch of motionless sleep. When I awoke, two words were written in sparkling silver-white letters on my white pillowcase: massage therapist.

It was a Thursday. I went to work, quit my job, and enrolled in an accelerated, nine-month medical massage program that started the following Tuesday. I graduated top of the class. I passed the State Medical Board licensing exam and started seeing clients on the third floor of my house because no one would hire me. I had no experience. So, I became an entrepreneur.

After two months, as one of my favorite clients was lying on my massage table, I sat at her head, finishing the massage session with a Reiki treatment, my hands hovering over her freckled shoulders. Fuzzy shapes were surrounding me.

Show yourself. I'm not afraid of you.

Nine figures standing on three sides of the table dressed in robes, cloaks, and hooded garments focused into view. They looked as if they were drawn with white charcoal pencils against the low lighting in the room. I looked at each one with wonder and curiosity. No breathing, no blinking, no grief, as if I could observe this mystical moment for an infinite amount of time. One pointed to my eyes, then to the space between my eyes on my forehead.

I was looking at them with the wrong eyes.

That was 11 years ago. Since then, through meditation, shamanic breathwork journeys, personal retreats, moments of stillness in nature, and the ability to stay open to all spiritual experiences with wonder and curiosity, I have established a connection with spirit guides, power animals, star beings, and galactic dragons. I see them, listen to them, and talk to them—both mine and my clients.'

You can, too. You can find your way to connect to spirits—seeing them, feeling their presence, hearing them, or sensing them in your own way, especially to the spirit of a loved one, either a person or animal. Shift from your body connecting to their body to your spirit connecting to their spirit. Trust yourself.

THE TOOL

This guided meditation can be used if a loved one is actively dying or has passed through the veil. Use it while holding their hand or in a comfortable place with their photo, talisman, or beloved object. If you would like me to walk through it with you, go to my YouTube channel: https://youtu.be/1tvcIrjMahQ

Trust yourself to find answers with clarity and confidence. Clarity comes from openness. Confidence comes from practice. Greet spiritual beings with wonder and curiosity. Trust the process. Know in your bones that you are protected and supported.

Prepare a solitary space that is comfortable—light a candle. Silence your phone. Take three breaths in through your nose and out of your mouth as if emptying your body of all thoughts, expectations, and future appointments. With each exhale, release what you can't control around you. Exhale slower and longer each time as if you could empty every cell in your body of stress.

Call to the four directions: your birth (East), your present moment (South), your future death (West), and your ancestors and spirit guides (North). Ask your higher power to hold a space of love and protection for you, surrounding you with golden light.

You are going to meet your loved one. Set the scene: Imagine a place, your favorite place in the world. Imagine every detail using all your senses:

What does this place look like? A cafe, a beach along a lake or ocean, a room.

What does it sound like? Are there other people, birds or animals, background noise?

What does it feel like? Is the sun on your skin, breeze in the air, shade from the heat of the day?

What does it taste like? Do you have a cold beverage to share, a picnic, a cup of tea?

Invite your loved one to join you. Bring him/her into your scene. Ask him/her to be with you.

Greet him/her with love and gratitude. Feel his/her presence. Hold his/her hand or touch him/her. Ask your questions. Have a conversation about your concerns and feelings. Imagine you have a thousand years to be together.

When it's time, come back to the present. Say goodbye for now. Hug him/her. Let him/her return to his/her spiritual home. Know that you can come back and be with him/her again soon. Send him/her with love in your heart.

Give yourself time to reflect and bring back the experience. Write about what you heard and saw in a journal. Drink water. Allow the experience to sit in your body. Stay quiet and listen for more messages from other spiritual guides around you.

If you are called to explore your spiritual path, remember that we are not meant to know the greater design, The Great Mystery. Have faith that you are on your right path with divine timing. Every experience is working for your highest and best outcome. You are loved and supported in more ways than you can possibly believe. Your spirit will rise to meet your path. You are inevitable.

I'm Atlantis Wolf. And I believe in you.

Atlantis Wolf is a Shamanic Life Coach and workshop leader who helps people seeking answers to their medical, spiritual, and emotional questions with the help of her spirit guides, power animals, and galactic dragons.

She grew up on a single-lane dirt road in the country, walking barefoot through the forest, whistling to birds, and wondering what she was supposed to do on Earth. She once blew her own mind watching the clock on the family stove move forward a tic and felt a flush of anxiety through her body. At an early age, she realized that a whole lifetime is a cosmic blink.

She lives like an oak tree with an equal number of branches reaching up to the light as those reaching down into the darkness—an equal amount of living above ground holding coaching sessions, workshops, and shamanic breathwork events, and below ground cultivating a vast interior landscape of gardens and spiritual healing temples. Her stories are in direct proportion to above as below. There are stories beneath her stories.

Above the ground, she was a girl who was told to follow in her family's footsteps to become an engineer instead of pursuing writing which was unlikely to have a lucrative future. She compromised by pursuing a dual major in civil engineering and English, minoring in environmental engineering. She has worked as a civil engineer, technical writer, business analyst, project manager, licensed medical massage therapist, marketing consultant, emotional release therapist, and entrepreneur. Below the ground, she was asleep until her mother's death awakened her gifts to see and communicate with spiritual beings and remember her past lives as an Egyptian healer, Toltec curandera, and Ayurvedic traveling shaman. She is the Dragon Medicine Woman.

Atlantis is a single mom with four kids and six cats. She lives on Turtle Island.

AtlantisWolf.com

DragonMedicineWoman@gmail.com

YouTube: Atlantis Wolf

CHAPTER 6

MYSTICAL SIGNS

LISTENING AND WATCHING FOR MESSAGES FROM THE OTHER SIDE

Sherry Burns, End-of-Life Doula, MA

Note: To protect the privacy of individuals in the following stories, all names are fictitious.

MY STORY

My first experience with receiving a sign from a loved one who had crossed over occurred when I was 32 years old. My friend Harold was 66 and died a year after learning he had metastatic liver cancer. Harold and I worked together, and I adored him like a father. He was well-read, well-traveled, and charmingly easy-to-laugh. He loved telling stories of his adventures around the globe while in the military. He often talked about his favorite place—the Seychelles. He implored me to make it a priority to go there. He swore it was the most beautiful place on Earth.

Harold's death shook my world. The office echoed with emptiness without him there. After the funeral, when it was time to leave the graveside, I uttered a plea to Harold: "Please come by and say hello now and then."

A few weeks later, I was perusing magazines at my favorite bookstore when an issue of *Islands* magazine caught my eye. I pulled it out to discover a spectacular beach scene on the cover and the headline, *The Seychelles*. I whispered, "Hi, Harold. Miss you. Thanks for saying hello."

Since that seminal encounter, signs from the other side occur more frequently, and I've witnessed hospice families and doula clients and families having similar visitations.

THE TOOL

Death is sacred. It and birth are the two most extraordinary transitions we will experience. And as such, by nature, it manifests and brings forth energies and powers that, while present to us in our everyday lives, are particularly purposeful and meaningful.

As a person's death journey begins unfolding, the veil thins, and the person and their loved ones and friends stand in a time of extraordinary grace, blessings, and spiritual opportunity.

Before we delve into signs, I want to give you some assurance if your initial reaction to this topic is, *Oh, I'm not a psychic nor a mystic. Never have been. I don't see ghosts or hear voices. This doesn't apply to me.* Know that there are hosts of entities on the other side, longing to communicate with us. So if you've never had such experiences before, how do you start now? Very simply—by stating your intention. Let the Universe know you are open and wanting to be aware, to tune in. Then be sure to express gratitude as new relationships with spiritual entities unfold.

What are mystical signs, and why do they happen?

Loosely defined, signs are communications from spiritual entities. They may be from angels, ancestors, loved ones who have transitioned, loved ones who are preparing to transition, ascended masters, spirit guides, and so on. They may take the form of dreams, synchronicities, experiences involving the senses (such as visions and voices), and even events in the physical realm.

From my experience, entities communicate to instruct, assure, console, assist, guide, and delight us. My Seychelles encounter made my heart happy and assured me that Harold was all right on the other side.

SYNCHRONICITIES

Synchronicity is defined as *the simultaneous occurrence of events that seem significantly related but have no discernible connection.* It is the startling coincidence of synchronicities that makes us stop and notice. And that is why spiritual entities often use them to communicate with us. They often are funny and playful.

I recently encountered a woman whose dear grandmother was nearing death. The doctors told Lisa and her grandmother death was imminent. Grandma came to Lisa's house for the remainder of her days. She was ready and not afraid. Lisa, on the other hand, was profoundly grief-stricken. She couldn't bear the thought of Grandma's death. Although Grandma grew weaker, had little appetite, and slept much of the time, she remained on this side and exceeded the doctor's prediction.

During this time, Lisa struggled with anticipatory grief, which overshadowed the time she had with Grandma. Also, during this time, Lisa and her daughters had frequent encounters with cardinals. They tapped on Lisa's motel window every morning while she was out of town on business. One landed on her daughter's car every day as she headed home from work. One daughter sadly hit a cardinal while driving. Lisa described the cardinals as stalking them.

"What do these synchronicities mean?" she asked anxiously. I replied that the cardinals were Grandma's way of giving Lisa a sign. With palpable persistence, Grandma was trying to get Lisa's attention to ensure she listened, learned, engaged, and fully experienced the sacred event that was unfolding. Grandma would be okay where she was going.

PHYSICAL EVENTS

Some spirits have the ability to manipulate objects in our physical realm to send signs. A nun friend of mine, Jenny, was extremely close to her older sister. They were from a large family, and one of the little indulgences they liked to share between just the two of them was potato chips. No one knew about this sister secret. When Jenny's sister died tragically in her twenties in a car accident, Jenny was devastated and inconsolable. She called out to her sister that she needed a sign that she was all right on the other side. A few weeks after the sister's death, one of the nuns approached Jenny out of the blue and handed her a bag of potato chips. No conversation. Just a bag of chips.

During a regularly scheduled visit with my favorite intuitive, she told me that a cat was on its way to me. Tara said to pay close attention lest I miss the sign. I brushed the comment off, as we were what I considered a full house with two cats. Then a few months later, my little soulmate cat died suddenly. She was only 12, and so I had thought we had many more years ahead of us together. I was blindsided and heartbroken when she died. My husband and I were in the middle of moving across the country and agreed we wouldn't get a new kitten until after the move. Despite that agreement, I still found myself perusing rescue kittens online and looking for a sign to guide me to THE ONE. I'd always wanted a Maine Coon, but Russian Blues kept coming up in my searches.

One brisk January day, I met up with friends at a park for a hike. As I pulled into the park, I saw my friends huddled together, grinning. Then I spotted a gray cat cuddled in one of their arms. They were sure it was meant to be mine. I told them we weren't getting a new cat until after the move. But secretly, I thought, *if the cat is still here when we get back from our hike, then perhaps this is the cat Tara told me about.*

When we returned from our hike an hour later, not only was the cat still there, but she saw us quite a distance away and came sprinting. Under my breath, I muttered, "I've been asking for a sign, but this timing isn't right." One of my friends heard and exclaimed, "You want a sign? What more of a sign could there be? A sweet cat apparently dumped in a park... and you wanted an adventure cat. Well, there's your adventure cat."

I knew she was right and laughed at my reticence despite all the obvious signs. After having the cat scanned to confirm there was no chip, posting all over social media to find her owners, and a wellness check, she joined our family. Her name is Pooja, which means *prayer* in Hindi.

DREAMS

When we sleep, our incarnated ego rests too, giving our spirits the freedom to journey and interact with other spirits. It's no wonder that mystical signs often come to us in the form of dreams.

Mr. Dawson was an elderly widower who enjoyed serving as an acolyte for mass on Sundays at the monastery where I lived. After mass, he loved coming to the reception room for breakfast to be doted upon by the older nuns. I don't know why, but this irritated me. He irritated me. Perhaps I was a little too proud of life in the cloister and didn't like outsiders getting too close.

One night I had a dream about Mr. Dawson. In it, I was his daughter. I received a call that he was gravely ill and in the hospital. I ran down hospital hallways in a frantic search to find him. A nurse pointed me to his room. I hesitantly opened the door and found him, not sickly and in bed, but vibrant and sitting in a chair by the window. Brilliant sunlight shone upon him through the window, making his silver hair a radiant crown. He turned to me with a smile and said, "Everything is going to be all right."

The next morning, as I headed to chapel for morning prayers, I found an announcement on the bulletin board that Mr. Dawson had died of a heart attack during the night. Given the negative feelings I had about him, why did he choose to visit me? (Granted, he probably visited many others.) It's a mystery I probably won't solve until it's my time to cross over, but I am touched that he visited, and the dream still gives me much to ponder.

VISIONS

Of all the ways spirits can communicate with us, visions can be unnerving if you're not accustomed to them. They may appear to be in the physical realm or in your mind's eye. Either way, they can be startling.

My adoptive father was diagnosed with Stage IV colon cancer in his early seventies. Scarcely a year after being diagnosed, the doctors said there was nothing more they could do, and we admitted him to hospice in-home care. Within a month, he grew extremely weak, and caring for him took a physical and emotional toll on my mother. We admitted him to inpatient hospice. During his last days, I often uttered in my mind, *be sure to come to say hello. Let us know you're okay.*

Dad died around 10:00 in the morning. As often happens with this event, many things started happening, seemingly out of our control. The nurse called the funeral home listed on Dad's admitting paperwork. CNAs arrived to bathe and dress in him a fresh, crisp hospital gown. The hospice chaplain arrived. Our heads were spinning as we responded to all the demands of the day. Things finally quieted down by evening, and we grabbed some food and took shelter in the quiet of what was now my mom's home.

Exhausted, she went to bed early. My mind was still reeling, and I found myself sitting in the dimly lit family room. No TV. No internet. Just space and time and thoughts. In an instant, an image flashed in my mind's eye.

I saw my dad as a young man. He didn't look like the man I had seen in photos all my life, but I knew it was him. He looked tired but strong. Standing at each side were feminine creatures that felt to me to be angels. They were placing an ornate robe on his shoulders. The robe was heavy fabric with gold epaulets at the shoulders. I knew intuitively that this was his victory robe. Certainly, my dad was human and far from perfect. Aren't we all? But he persevered. He lived life fully, flaws and scars and all. He gave it his best shot, and he was a victor.

I think about this vision often—what a gift. It assures me not only that Dad is fine on the other side but that we all will be when it's our time.

VOICES

Voices, like visions, can be a bit unnerving. So often people who hear voices are judged to be mentally unwell. But there are numerous genius minds who heard voices—Carl Jung, Sigmund Freud, Samuel Beckett, and Mahatma Gandhi, to name a few.

Although the following story isn't related to a death, it's an example of both asking for a sign and of how answers to such requests can be delivered.

For a few years, I managed a small department at a manufacturing company. One of the people on the team was a woman, Danielle, in her early twenties. She was a team player, worked hard, and seemed to have an active lifestyle. Despite this, there was an air of restlessness about her. It seemed to me like she was searching for something.

One morning, as I brushed my teeth, I heard, "Tell Danielle to go to library school." The voice was so real it startled me, and I looked around expecting to see someone in the bathroom with me.

When Danielle arrived at work that morning, I approached her tentatively. "Morning, Danielle. Um. I'm supposed to give you a message."

She looked at me curiously. "A message?"

"Yes. You're supposed to go to library school."

Danielle started to cry. Neither one of us could speak for a while, and then she broke the silence. "I've been praying for months for a sign as to what I should do with my life. Library school is so right. I don't know how I didn't think of it myself. Thank you so much for telling me." We hugged—she out of happiness, me out of relief that she didn't think I might have lost my mind. A month or two later, I provided a letter of recommendation for her application to a Master of Library Science program at a nearby university. No, I did not mention the voice.

INTERPRETING MYSTICAL SIGNS

The meaning of a sign may not be as immediately obvious as the Seychelles on the cover of *Islands* magazine or Mr. Dawson seated in radiant light. They often are symbolic, like my dad's victory robe. The interpretation of archetypes and symbols is a profound study—one that psychologists, psychiatrists, religious, mystics, and everyday people like you and me have been pondering for centuries. That said, here are a few questions you can ask yourself to help interpret the meaning of symbols you encounter:

What emotions did I feel?

The emotions that a symbol evokes will tell you much about its meaning. What did the unknown soldier in your dream arouse? Fear, courage, memories of the father you miss? Perhaps you asked the Universe to give you a sign about whether you should travel around the globe to see your dying grandmother, and a playful corgi, just like your grandmother's, appears in your mind's eye, evoking joy.

When I saw my father being robed by angels, I felt his fatigue, relief, satisfaction, sense of completion. I also felt awe at the sight of him being robed.

Certainly, many objects in signs are archetypes that have universal meaning, and it's enriching to research and understand those, but signs are personal, and what matters most is what the object means to you. Pondering the emotions it evokes is essential to uncovering the message. Positive emotions, such as joy, affection, and hope, may indicate affirmation. Negative ones, such as anger, frustration, and embarrassment, may be telling you to change course.

What does the person mean to me?

Dreams and visions where a dying person appears can either be a visitation from that soul or a symbol to convey a message to you. People in our dreams may symbolize that part of ourselves. So to interpret the sign, ask yourself what this person means to you. Are they a wise, supportive father figure; a fun-loving friend; a friend you've made bad choices with while hanging out together? That person's meaning for you represents that part of you.

I once dreamed that I was on a journey with a close friend. In it, Jean and I wandered through remote villages, and she taught me how to buy and send cards back home to my loved ones. The only emotions in the dream were the slightest bit of frustration at apparently being a slow learner.

From the moment I met Jean, I knew that her primary soul gift was divine love. It exudes from her every pore. An intuitive once told me that divine love was one of my soul gifts too, but well below my primary and secondary gifts. I was skeptical. I see someone like Jean, and I don't see that kind of unconditional warmth in myself. So, if in the dream Jean represents that part of me, my higher self is teaching me about gestures of love and care.

What do the objects and events in the dream mean to me?

In my dream with Jean, I was traveling across the countryside from village to village. In real life, yes, I'm a traveler, but I understood the dream to be about life's journey. It was about going from place to place, accompanied by someone wise, teaching me life lessons.

As you analyze symbols and acquire a collection of interpretations, it can be fun and helpful to compile a symbol dictionary. I keep mine in the back of my dream journal, referring to it often and finding fun in reminiscing.

CONCLUSION

Accompanying and providing care for a dying loved one, or even a stranger can be beyond painful and wrenching. As a caregiver, you may find yourself reaching deeper than you knew possible to find emotional muscle and resources for this journey. Know that you are surrounded by loving, supportive spirits. Call out for their palpable and observable support, and then lean your heart in to hear and see.

Sherry Burns is a wife, mother, and avid traveler, reader, and foodie. She was born in South Korea and moved to the States when her father's tour of duty with the army ended. In terms of ethnicity, she is Korean, Hispanic, and Native American, topped off with a little European. This mix of genes is elemental to her identity and outlook.

In her twenties, Sherry was a semi-cloistered, contemplative nun, spending her days studying and meditating. These were formative years that influenced her spiritual journey and led her to the study of world religions and beliefs in a quest to formulate her own.

Sherry lives in Santa Fe, New Mexico, with her husband and two ridiculous cats. In the spring of 2019, Sherry retired as a director for a medical software company, working in product design and development.

Throughout her adult life, Sherry has been intrigued with death and dying—the physical and biological processes, cultural expression, and spiritual and emotional experiences. She is a hospice volunteer, supporting families and patients and specifically sitting vigil with patients whose families or friends are unable to be present as they transition.

The growing shift in Western culture towards reclaiming ownership of the death journey inspired Sherry to become an end-of-life doula. Empowering people to create their own self-directed transition and accompanying them on their journey is a profound privilege. She completed her end-of-life doula training through the University of Vermont, Larner College of Medicine. As a doula, Sherry hosts Death Cafes and is active in legislation, both locally and nationally, to evolve and enhance laws regarding death practices and the disposition of the body.

Visit Sherry at https://sherryburns.org/ and https://www.facebook.com/sherryburns.eold.

CHAPTER 7
TRUST THE PROCESS

HOLDING SACRED SPACE

Lisa Karasek, Quantum Healer

MY STORY

I remember talking to my first ghost while I was still in the crib. When I was a teenager, I had conversations with them in public, and then very clearly to me, they would walk away and disappear. You'll hear me tell stories about those times I would give someone directions, and I would get asked, "who are you talking to?" The truth is, I can see them in human form. But it wasn't until I was well into adulthood and took my first spiritual development class that I learned I am a healer. I asked my teacher, "what am I doing when I speak to them, then watch them go into the light?" She smiled and told me I have the gift for healing and that I can help souls cross over. Those souls were coming to me to teach me. After taking more classes and training to be an intuitive and spiritual practitioner, I learned I could do more and with purpose.

One day I was on the phone with a friend. He interrupted the conversation and apologized, saying, "I'm sorry, but I have to go. I just got a text that my father had a stroke and is being taken to the hospital." I asked my friend quickly what his father's name was. Instantly, I was able to connect with the father's energy. Intuitively I was given information about what could help him in the hospital. I shared the details with my friend, and he was able to use them. My friend told me the next day that I may have saved his father's life. The nurse did as I suggested and in critical time. Over the next couple of days, I continued to connect and receive intuitive information. I was able to feel into the many different ways he felt guilt, and I was able to help his soul heal those guilty emotions.

Recently, I was working with a new client who was in her golden years. She sought me out specifically for spiritual guidance and for what she could do to fulfill her purpose before it was too late. Together we did guided journeys. She was able to explore her deep desires, where outside influences were dissuading her, and where she felt most curious about things. We had discussions around what she felt good about in her life's work and where any regrets or confusion might be. These sessions helped her understand a little better where she felt aligned with herself and what spirit might be asking her to look at. She had a better understanding of what she could focus on to feel fulfilled before she no longer could. I learned shortly after working with her that she had passed.

A very good friend of mine who supports me as a healer asked if I would work with her father. He had been ill for a long time, years actually, and was almost in a catatonic state. She had him living with her to care for him easily, so it was comfortable for both of them during that time. He seemed to reach a point where he was no longer living but existing, and she was genuine in her concern: "Why isn't he dying?" I began with a basic chakra cleansing and body scan when he suddenly began communicating with me telepathically. My strongest skill as an intuitive is called claircognizance or knowing. Intuitive information comes to me in the form of thoughts as truth. My natural abilities as a healer allow me to work in different dimensions. And so we began a conversation that could not be heard physically, but that was between our souls. I learned he needed help with certain things before he was able to cross over. He had soul lessons and karmic contracts to complete. He was also doing healing work from his life's experiences. Luís was in his physically catatonic state because he was working hard in another dimension.

I prioritized working with Luís. Every day I sat in silence wherever I was and connected with him and gave him healing. We worked on his needs by way of telepathic communication. Ours were guidance sessions. Afterward, I would call my friend, check in, and ask her, "how is he doing today?" "He's awake a bit more, and we can talk a little bit. He is in much better spirits." Luís came to me one last time and asked me to get his daughter. He was ready, and he wanted her by his side. I thanked him for allowing me such a rewarding experience with him, and I called my friend on the phone and gave her her father's wish. She called me later that day to let me know that, yes, he did pass that afternoon. She was very thankful for the work I did with him, for making their last weeks together more informed and pleasurable. My work with her father allowed her to relax and not worry so much. It was consoling for her that he was doing important work that was of his highest good. We learned why he wasn't able to pass for all those months. And my friend was most comforted in knowing that her dying father was not in pain. For a few months after his passing, I continued to communicate with Luís and gave his daughter loving messages from him and her mother. In fact, he is communicating with me now, helping me to write this chapter.

THE TOOL

I have learned that just because someone else's final days don't look like we think they should, it doesn't mean they're doing it wrong. It also doesn't mean something is wrong with them.

We all have work to do while we are here. As we grow up, engage in family, social, and work relationships, have careers, and fail and succeed at things, we are doing soul work. There is spiritual work, as well as healing, for every one of us to attain. As we approach our time, this is when we can most see through the veil (the other dimension our soul operates in). Meaning, our souls are motivated to do the work each of our bodies is responsible for. We are all comprised of more than one body: we each have a physical body, an ethereal body, a spiritual body, an emotional body, and a mental body. Each of these different bodies has different responsibilities. The work and healing our different bodies do during life can be traced to, and for, a variety of reasons. The reasons may include work from our ancestors and present and past life traumas; for ourselves or for others. It could be that we are in the best position to, or have the best resources to do the work or healing now.

TRUST THE PROCESS

One of the best things you can do is not take anything personally. What you believe death and dying should look like may not support the process your loved one is going through. My guess is your loved one didn't know before now what their soul work and karmic work was, and you won't either. So especially don't force your fears, concerns, beliefs or opinions, or timelines on the dying. Only they and the universe knows what needs to be done now. By not having expectations, you will not add pressure, guilt, or shame for either one of you (or anyone else). Try as best you can and allow the process to be as organic as it can be. Remember, life and death are divinely timed, and everything is happening exactly as it is supposed to be.

Also, don't think that you can force any two people's dying processes to be similar or the same. What works for one person may not be what another person needs. Do your best to make important decisions based on their wants. Depending on where or how the dying is (lucid or not, critical or not), be respectful of what they would want and need at this time. Try not to let your emotions lead (or the siblings, or the cousins), or risk turning the experience into a drama that will forever go down as the big family story.

When the veil is thin, we see and feel the life energy differently. Now is the time to have the important conversations you want to with them. Chances are you will both gain new perspectives and insights and learn what needs to be learned from the conversation. You can ask specifically what they want for their body in an emergency, especially if they become unconscious and cannot speak for themselves. You may want to tell them how much you love them and why. You may want to share something you've been holding onto, something you've been afraid to share, or missed sharing. It's never too late to repair strained relationships. This may be part of the work they needed to complete. Or maybe, is it yours?

HOLD SPACE FOR THEM

Do everything at this time from the place of love. If you struggle with any parts of it, make it about them, not you. What is it they need right now to feel safe, supported, and loved? And provide it. If you aren't sure, remember to come back to trusting the process. When you can relax, it lets them know that no matter what, everything is going to be okay. They will relax into their experience and process too. Their souls are working for their highest good and their highest power.

Lisa Karasek, three-time bestselling Amazon author, expert Quantum Healer, TRE® Certified Facilitator, and Certified Eating Psychology Coach. Lisa is able to update her client's states of being to assist in healing using ancient, multi-dimensional healing and Holistic Metamorphosis® (an angelic energy healing modality), consciousness-based practices, and TRE® (tension and trauma releasing exercises). Lisa powerfully guides her clients to a healthier, happier, and more purposeful life.

Lisa Karasek is dedicated and passionate about helping you work with the dynamics of your self-relationship and believes this is the key to most Mind Body Spirit disease and illness. Find more information about her and her programs at www.LisaKarasek.com

Amazon Author Page: https://www.amazon.com/Lisa-Karasek/e/B087W4BYS7/ref=ntt_dp_epwbk_4

Facebook: https://www.facebook.com/LisaMKarasek

Telegram: https://t.me/MindBodySpiritGuidanceLK

Schedule: https://LisaKarasek.10to8.com

CHAPTER 8

YOUR PATH IS REVEALED

TRANSFORMING FROM CAREGIVING TO SELF-CARING

R. Scott Holmes, Usui Reiki Master, Polarity Therapist

MY STORY

My wife of thirty-nine years turned slowly, painfully in bed—her bruised, chemo-battered and misshapen body in pain with every movement in the hot August night. I gently placed my hand on her hip, trying not to cause her any pain. All the while, I was desperately trying to hold back the tears, not wanting to share the depth of my sadness.

I always felt I needed to keep my emotions in check, being the superhero with cape unfurled, flying in to save the day, the week, or the moment. And here she was comforting me. "We will get through this together like we have every other time."

Tough spots were nothing new to us. Married when we were nineteen and twenty, three daughters in five years, it was a struggle. Moira took care of the house and kids while finishing her teaching degree. I worked two to three jobs to make enough to provide. It was tough, but together we worked hard at it.

Then the day came when our lives changed forever. Moira called me at work, "Something is wrong with Amanda; she woke up from her nap, and she won't respond to us." Our daughter was in a trance-like state. Being fifteen months old and the youngest meant she was the most energetic and engaging of our three daughters. But my wife and neighbor could not get her to respond to any stimuli. "Meet me at the pediatrician's office; I'm calling right now."

I raced to the office ten minutes away. Walking into the overflowing waiting room, I walked over to where Moira was cradling Amanda. There was a slight twitch in the corner of Amanda's mouth. I immediately picked her up and led Moira to the doctor's in-door, telling the staff she was starting to seize. Within five minutes, both doctors on duty and the nurse were doing what they could to calm down a grand mal seizure in a child with no symptoms or history of any disorder.

"We are sending her to Floating Hospital in Boston," Dr. Hourigan said. I looked at Moira's wide, fear-filled eyes and knew our little girl was in real trouble. The ambulance ride into Boston at rush hour, the hours waiting and not knowing what was going on, the first time hearing our perfectly happy, healthy daughter cry, truly cry, was devastating.

Two days later, as we finally left the hospital, Amanda was in the Pediatric ICU with a bolt in her head to measure cranial pressure, an A-line in her thigh, and not much hope she would survive the week. She was diagnosed with Herpes Encephalitis Simplex 2, a virus that devastates and destroys parts of the brain. It stopped just short of killing her. Going home was the most important thing we had to do that day, as my two other daughters had essentially lost their sister and their parents as we were taking care of Amanda. We needed to reassure them that however scared we might be, they would be okay.

Three months later, Amanda was transferred to our local hospital. Two weeks later, we had our daughter, still comatose, at home. We were scared out of our minds but determined to give her the best chance of survival and the best quality of life.

Two years of Moira raising three daughters, one of whom was totally dependent on us with twenty-four-hour care with minimal outside help, put us up against the hardest decision we would have to make, allowing the state of Massachusetts to certify her for one of 260 pediatric nursing home beds, one of only two states at the time that had such facilities. It was best for our other girls and for us as they were starting school. And it was best for Amanda to get the care she needed as she grew older. We did not want to give her up, but the best chance for the highest quality of life for us all was to give up her everyday care.

This didn't stop us from taking the forty-five-minute ride two to three times a week to ensure all her needs were being met. We did her laundry, filled her bed with dozens of stuffed animals, brought her sisters to visit every week, and answered the middle of the night calls telling us she was sick and going to the local hospital in Plymouth, Massachusetts. The only problem was that the doctors did not know her complicated medical history. Amanda needed an advocate, as many times she was transferred into the major medical facilities in Boston. We did indeed get the grand tour of all those world-class hospitals.

The caregiving never stops when you have a multi-handicapped child. No matter the time of day or the obstacles in place, you answer the call.

Moira had a baseline mammogram at thirty-eight years old, as her mother had passed from ovarian cancer ten years earlier. The radiologist found a pencil point tumor up against her chest wall. Her worst fears were confirmed.

Months later, tears streamed down her face as long strands of her beautiful shoulder-length hair clumped out in her hands. Healing from the mastectomy, bloating and nausea were her constant companions, And yet, she always smiled, took care of the house, the kids, and her classroom until she was too weak to teach at school.

She made an impressive recovery, and we were thankful such a small tumor was found in time. Life started to get on an even keel when we got a call at two o'clock in the morning, expecting the nursing home letting us know Amanda was taking another trip to the hospital.

Instead, they told us that our fifteen-year-old daughter had died. Quietly, peacefully and without pain. Driven to the hospital by our good friends, we identified our little girl in the darkened hospital room, asking them not to perform an autopsy, as she had gone through so much in her short life, we would add no more scars but would carry our own scars in our hearts.

Moira experienced twenty-two years of chemotherapy, radiation, FDA studies, experimental radiation for tumors that had metastasized to her liver, more chemo, and more pills than anyone should ever have to take. All of this while she pursued her love of teaching elementary school, keeping house, doting on our daughters then grandchildren, losing her biggest cheerleader, her dad, constant oversight and tests at Boston's Mass General Hospital Breast Cancer Clinic, and week-long stays in the oncology wing. The cancer would abate, then grow again, but her smile, warm, caring heart, and quirky humor were always on display until they weren't. Job changes and early, forced retirement became long days reclining in the La-Z-Boy. She was diminishing, dwindling, becoming smaller. Moira then became what she never was, a cancer patient, when she had always been "someone with cancer."

I held Moira through that night in August 2016. We were warriors going into battle against an unrelenting foe, knowing that very soon, she wouldn't be there. "I'm scared," she whispered, further shattering my heart. After an hour of holding and comforting, I kissed her on the forehead, held her face to mine, and said, "You're not dying tonight. We'll make the best of whatever time we have left."

Six weeks later, I coaxed and carried her down the stairs from our bedroom for the last time, settling her into the hospital bed, now in our living room. We made a pact; no hospitals, no nursing home, no extraordinary means. She was to stay home with family, period.

For two weeks, family and friends came to visit as the Hospice nurses tended to her increased pain and physical needs, someone always by her bedside within hand-holding distance. For ten days, she held on without food or water, just pain meds, and when it became almost unbearable to observe, she passed away, gasping, with my oldest daughter holding her hand. The wake and funeral were a blur, stretching out in time, yet gone in a flash. I felt lost, cast adrift, not knowing what I should be doing or feeling or whether I could get out of bed.

The only thing anchoring me were my daughters, but they had responsibilities and families of their own. A month later, I went back to work in that somnambulistic way of putting one foot in front of another without much thought or understanding. *How could I get through the day not being responsible for my wife, all of her needs, maintaining everything as she would like it? How?*

The stillness in the house was so loud it hurt my ears. Our cat did not enjoy long conversations and had limited interests. TV was mindless. So when a friend offered a ticket to see a local medium, I thought, *what could it hurt?* I had never been to such an event. The 350 other guests all thought it was a great idea also. At least I got out of the house for the night. Not expecting anything to happen, I was shocked that the medium asked me to stand up and gave me the guest microphone in the last fifteen minutes. It seems that my daughter Amanda wanted to come through and let me know she was wonderful, marvelous, doing somersaults, and full of bright energy even though in life she was multi-handicapped.

"She wants you to know she's always with you, by your side watching over you," the medium told me as she moved to the other side of the room. Flabbergasted and choking on the tears streaming down my face, she interrupted her other reading and said, "Amanda wants you to get your tire fixed and stop just putting air in it!" I had a bad front tire and was waiting until the weekend to fix it. I became a true believer that night, and I've never looked back.

Cleaning out my house of everything I didn't need, while heartbreaking, was cathartic. I smiled at pictures of the life Moira and I built, our family, as well as things we had collected over the years. What I came to realize was I truly didn't need much to survive or function. Out went half the furniture in the house, out went anything not used or worn in five years, out went the save-just-in-case things. I was cleaning my house, but more importantly, was tending to myself, weeding my garden of the weight of material things, feeling lighter by the day.

Possibilities blossomed. I took a Reiki One course. Then Reiki Two. As I had always been interested in massage, I went to a local school and found that they taught Polarity Therapy as well. Changing my work schedule to accommodate night classes, I went to school three nights a week for four months. The work infused me with energy, satiating my curiosity and enriching my life with an understanding that my life is what I make of it. In order to change the world, it starts with me.

Each modality I participated in brought a higher understanding and more skills at moving energy, feeling the unseen, and being in a position to help people. I had found a way to take my caregiving skills and turn them into self-caring skills. The world of light, laughter, and compassion opened for me and keeps me in awe. I am thankful and loved by my two angels that sit on my shoulders, every moment, every day, reminding me how magnificent life can be.

THE TOOL

The loved one you've cared for, cried over, fought with, and held up is gone. And now you have no idea how to move through each day without first checking their schedule, seeing to their needs, or checking with their doctors and prescriptions; in short, how to start living, again.

The first step is stillness. Call it meditation, quiet time, reflection, or vegging out. This is when you need to reacclimate to quiet, not having the next 17 hours scheduled or filled for you. It can be scary and disorienting at first. This is where you come back to the present, slow down, feel your adrenaline dissipate as you're no longer on that roller coaster, feeling like you can never stop moving,

The focus is you, even if it's for only twenty minutes each day. Make that time a priority, *the* priority. It's how you start to heal, creating and clearing the space within you.

Get back into your body. After the stress and traumas of long-term caregiving, you need to find that sweet spot in your physical health where rest, strength, and stamina are in sync. Use your diet, take your vitamins, get a massage, use oils, do yoga, climb a tree, lift two pounds, five pounds, one hundred pounds, walk, do yardwork; whatever feels good; just move.

You'll find what seemed overwhelming isn't, like getting out of bed; it becomes the first step to the rest of your day. Emphasis on steps as better moods, more positive thoughts, and better decisions make a comeback.

Acknowledge your feelings as they come up, the good, the bad, and the ugly. They are all valid, acceptable, reasonable, and a part of who you are. If it helps, this is where journaling, even if it's only a few words, comes in. Get the thoughts and feelings out of your head and heart. Look them in the eye and tell those feelings you see them. Clearly, some days, overwhelming on others, but know those sentiments are there.

These parts of you—anger, sadness, love, fear, joy, shame, judgment— and the relationship you had or wished you had with your loved one are all there, needing acknowledgment and understanding.

Forgiveness. Caregivers forgive their loved ones, but have you forgiven yourself? Remember that time your anger got the better of you at 2:00 in the morning with no sleep? Remember being impatient because they couldn't or wouldn't do something needed? Know in your heart you did the best you could under the circumstances. You are not and cannot be perfect. Stress, sleep deprivation, worry, and the unknown in any situation do not allow us to be our best selves.

I've often thought back to a situation and wished I had been more caring or shown more understanding and compassion than I did. You did your best. Allow the same caring and forgiving attitude you used to take care of someone else to surround and take care of you.

Find what brings you joy. Who can you talk with or sit with for hours (my grandchildren) that brings you unlimited joy? Remember what that feels like. Maybe your joy is climbing that hill in the woods, riding a bike for the first time in so many years, taking three hours to read beside a pond, picking up your instrument for the first time in years, going to lunch in the middle of the week with a close friend, going through your long lost pine cone collection, finishing that long put-off project, or finding that thing within you that brings a smile.

Your healing journey has begun. Reconnecting with friends and family after so much time consumed with caregiving may feel awkward at first. You've put other priorities first, lost connections to those closest to you. Open up the lines of communication, reestablish those relationships and feel some more of that weight you've been carrying fall away. This is for your continued journey to becoming you again.

Lastly, take your time. No one should put a limit or timetable on grieving. Those pictures that were so hard to look at two months ago may bring a smile when shared with family. Talking about the memories, funny times, scary nights, and oh-my-God moments helps you to heal. The pain and sadness are there, sometimes rolling over you like you're drowning, sometimes making you laugh, but it serves to keep you on the path to finding you again.

Whatever your journey, you will become more self-aware and more compassionate with yourself and your relationships. You feel lighter, more energized, and ready to live joyfully. Welcome back! This is the start of the best parts of your life.

Scott Holmes is a Reiki Master, Polarity Therapist, RYSE teacher, and Theta Healer living south of Boston, Massachusetts. His journey through loss and caregiving has allowed the healing tools we all possess to come to fruition. His practice is a mixture of modalities that allow healing on the emotional, spiritual, physical, and energetic planes.

If you are disappointed, disillusioned, unhappy, or angry about the current state of your life and know in your heart you deserve a full and joyous life, we can start the journey to fulfillment. Are you motivated, inspired, and willing to do the work necessary to uncover, heal and remove the blocks that prevent you from moving forward?

Chakra clearing, Inner child healing, Chord clearing, Belief transformation, Inner male and female realignment, Energetic flow, Self-realization, Meditation, Crystals, Therapeutic oils, and Acupressure are all tools used to help transform those things that no longer serve you.

You are a divine spiritual being of light and love. You have as much right as anyone for joy and success. Allow yourself to become your highest and best, with grace and ease, finding compassion within you. Your healing journey begins here to help rediscover the purpose you were put on this earth for.

If you want to move forward on your journey, start your journey, or renew your journey, contact me at:

Website: rscottholmes.com

Email: rscott_holmes@yahoo.com

CHAPTER 9

IMMORTALITY IS YOUR TRUE HOME

MEDITATION ON THE KNOWER CAN GET YOU THERE

Dr. Shelley Astrof

MY STORY

Did you ever think you could live forever?

You can connect with your immortal home through meditation on the Knower, your immortal soul.

I heard it said that home is where the heart is. I'll always think of my grandmother as being my first true home.

I spent my early years with my grandmother. With her, I always felt safe and loved. She was my shelter from the bumps and bruises of the outside world. We had an extraordinary bond. She believed I was her daughter who died after she came to the new world. Poverty stole this child from her. I was her second chance, and she poured her precious gifts into me.

She often talked about God. "God is everywhere, *mein kindt*. You must create your own personal relationship with God."

"Bubby, how do I do that?"

"Every night, repeat the prayer *kriyas shema*."

I never disclosed our private conversations. They were our sacred moments. That was why it wasn't until I was in my 20s that I discovered I had misheard my grandmother's words.

My young ears misheard the name of the Hebrew prayer *kriyas shema*. As it turned out, from the age of three or four, every night, I prayed to *Krishna*, "*Krishna, Krishna, Krishna.*"

It makes me giggle to think I spent all those years praying to the deity known for imparting the knowledge of immortality to his beloved companion Arjun in the famous Indian scripture, the Bhagavad Gita. A foreshadowing of my life to come.

My grandmother died when I was eleven. During her final days, I would wake up in the middle of the night and crawl into bed with her. "Bubby, I'm scared."

Every night she comforted me with the exact same words. She rarely used my name; mostly, she referred to me as *mein kindt*, my child. "I'll always love you. I'll always look after you. I'll never leave you. Even if you don't see me, you have to know this."

The night she died, I didn't wake up.

I thought a lot about her final words, every fiber of my being knew she spoke the truth. But there was much my mind had to understand about this life and death thing.

My grandmother had just departed, and my mother was pregnant. Birth and death were on my mind. *Does life become life only when a child is born? Does life die when the body is dead? Is existence dependent only on a body?*

My life took a very different turn after my grandmother's passing. I had to adjust to living with my family. It never felt like home.

The next time I felt that sense of home was when I met my guru.

Just seeing his photo for the first time, I knew he was my home. Staring at his picture, I felt that love, safety, and quiet joy that I had only ever felt with my grandmother. It was as if I could breathe deep again with the sense that everything is really all right.

Through that profound experience of seeing his photo, I knew I had seen the purpose of my life. It would take many more years for my mind and my life to catch up to what I experienced at that moment.

The meaning of guru comes from two words: *gu* meaning darkness or ignorance, and *ru* meaning remover. In other words, guru refers to the one who removes your darkness or ignorance and thereby reveals the light, the knowledge of enlightenment.

I remember how extraordinary it was for me to meet him on my first visit to India. All the cells in my body tingled with that sense of awakening as my conscious awareness heightened. I felt like a star exploding, shooting out rays of light, sparkling, dancing, and glowing with the brilliance of the sun. I knew I was standing near the embodiment of the source of that spectacular light. I knew he was my home.

I learned from him that there is a technique to reach that space of home. It's through the practice of meditation on the Knower, your original self or soul.

"If you want to know your immortal nature," he would say, "then you have to learn the difference between what changes and what doesn't. Your mind changes, your body changes, your senses change, your situations and circumstances change. What is it that doesn't change? There is something inside you that witnesses the changes. That something is always there. It never changes. It is eternal and goes by the name Knower. It was there before the body was born and will be there after the body is gone. It is also there in between."

He always advised, "This body is your only tool to reach your goal, so respect it and keep it healthy. Body-wise we are all different. But there is something that is not the body that is also me." It has many names in Sanskrit, *ātmā, chetan, brahm*; in English, it's called the Knower.

Every day, he held an open forum, a gathering called *satsang*, which means the company of truth. In this case, the word truth means the original unchanging, immortal being opposite to the manifest forms, both physical and subtle, that change—the body, mind, and senses.

I remember sitting in *satsang* listening with rapt attention to his spontaneous, humorous expression that always brought so much joy and laughter to the most profound and subtle philosophy, the knowledge of the unchanging.

He never referred to anyone as followers or disciples. He always maintained that we were would-be Gurus or would-be masters.

He would often say things like, "The mind doesn't know the Knower because it has no legs, no eyes, no ears, no conclusion, no intellect, no ego, no mind, no senses, no name, and no form. That's why you're not convinced of the Knower. So, close your eyes and let your mind and senses settle down. Your habit is believing that you live in the body, and since the body dies, you think that you die. Focus on who is watching. That is you, the Knower, pure, free, forever, immortal, and unborn."

To release the mind from that which binds it to uneasiness, he suggested the importance of using mantra in meditation "Repeat the mantra *amaram hum madhuram hum*, I am immortal, I am blissful, or I am pure, free, forever. The mantra is talking to you, the Knower who is immortal. And remember, anything that dies is not immortal."

I remember when he suggested that I study the Bhagavad Gita. About forty years ago, the sun was blazing hot one early afternoon; I sat beside him on a platform as he gazed at me with intensity. It felt like I was being x-rayed from the inside out. He said, "You should study the Bhagavad Gita. It really is your book." Suddenly, I felt this cool breeze move through me. Then came the excitement of this incredible directive. It all felt so right.

I started to read the Gita and totally related to the story. On the surface, it's about this dysfunctional family who ends up at war with each other. The Bhagavad Gita actually takes place on a battlefield. I could relate. It always felt like I was at war with my family.

But as the years went on and I started to look past the intricately woven storylines, I began to enter its depths. I realized that the Gita is a promise from Krishna, the name I misheard as a Hebrew prayer oh so many years before. Krishna is the personification of the immortal, original self, the Knower state of consciousness. He is guiding his own dear mind Arjun towards enlightenment. It's a guidebook on how to reach your true immortal home, the Knower of you really are.

The Bhagavad Gita, also known as the Song Celestial, is a Sanskrit poem that's often sung. I spent many years studying the magnificent verses that guide the mind to understand its true home, its immortal Knower state.

I love to deconstruct the Sanskrit verses and then put them back together with a fresh understanding of the eternal and immortal and the changing and illusory. I also had the tremendous opportunity to be able to ask for clarity and guidance.

The Song Celestial discusses the distinction between our transitory, changeable material world and its unchanging, immortal, underlying nature, called the home of all. Krishna lets Arjun know that the eternal state of consciousness is attainable as he guides his own mind towards this monumental goal.

In one of my favorite verses, Krishna gently guides his mind, Arjun, to know his truth as immortality. He helps Arjun understand that bodies and forms change, and the space of the Knower is forever unchanging.

In this verse, Krishna tells Arjun that the underlying manifestation of form is the eternal Knower. While it dwells in the body, it witnesses childhood, youth, old age, and death and then assumes another body form. Krishna reminds him that the changes happen on the level of the body. The Knower remains forever and unchanging. The one who knows this is wise.

I've come to know that the mind always sees dualistically. It understands according to pairs of opposites—hot and cold, good and bad, birth and death. When I meditate, the space of the infinite Knower is carried to the mind. During meditation, the world of the mind doesn't exist to bind me as I am attending the life, the soul, the Knower, which has no form. My mind knows life only with form, but in meditation, I know life without the help of the changing mind because I know life with my being.

THE TOOL

I am offering three tools to enhance your experience of the Knower state of consciousness, your true home. They are all available on the resource page of my website: knower.ca/resources

1. A VISUALIZATION: THE ORIGINAL HOME OF AN EARTHEN CUP

Take your time to read this through, think about it, and be the observer of this visualization.

In India, some tea stalls still serve their delicious chai in unglazed earthenware.

Imagine a mound of earth. Watch as the potter reaches his hand into the cold, damp ground to grab a handful of clay.

The mound of earth is the universal element from which all earthenware forms are made. The universal element is comparable to the universal consciousness. The Knower, like the earth, is there before any form comes into existence. They are the original home of forms.

When the potter separates a handful of clay from the mound of earth, it is still earth; it is just individual earth. Just like the individual, Knower or soul is a distinctly separate and unique part of consciousness. The soul has not become anything else; it's simply individual.

The potter takes the individual handful of earth and begins to shape it into the form of a cup. The individual soul begins to take on a material body. As the cup is baked in the kiln, the material form of consciousness takes the shape of a body. When the form appears, we call it birth.

The cup has not become something other than earth, just as the body has not become something other than Knower consciousness.

The earthen cup has experiences and lives out its time, as does the human form.

One day the cup is broken. Some say the cup returned to the earth. The cup, however, was always earth, even while it held the shape of a cup. When the cup is broken, we might say that the form of the cup died.

But it is only the form that has changed. The indweller or soul of the form has never changed. It is still its originality, be it earth or Knower consciousness.

Once again, the potter reaches into the mound of earth for a handful of clay.

We can know our true home by tuning in to our original state of conscious awareness, the Knower.

2. KNOWER MEDITATION

Make a comfortable seat and close your eyes.

Whenever you move to the deeper side of your understanding, you don't use your waking state mind that only knows things and forms on the outside.

Close your eyes and go inside. Let your mind be free from its regular thinking patterns.

Begin attending your breath; watch as you breathe in and breathe out. The movement of the breath is linked to the activity of the mind.

Pay attention to your incoming and outgoing breath. Think about what happens after you breathe out and before you breathe in. You'll notice that there is a pause before the breath changes direction. Pay attention to that pause as you continue to watch the movement of your breath.

Through watching your breath, the mind becomes part of it. Then there is no sense of division between you, your mind, and your breath. Attend the breath for a few moments.

Introduce the mantra "I am pure, free, forever" or *amaram hum madhuram hum*. Repeat the mantra inside your mind "I am pure, free, forever. I am pure, free, forever. I am pure, free, forever."

Through repetition of the mantra, your mind becomes absorbed in its true nature as you come to know that "I am pure, free, forever. I am pure, free, forever. I am pure, free, forever."

Attending the mantra sets the mind free from its routine conditioning. Pay attention to its meaning. "I am pure, free, forever. I am pure, free, forever. I am pure, free, forever."

As you repeat the mantra, watch how sometimes you are repeating the mantra; sometimes the mantra is lost, and sometimes you become aware that it's lost. The moment you become aware, know that you are the Knower.

Whenever you transcend, there is no mind at all, no sense of duality. The mind cannot bind your freedom when you are at home. When the mind reaches the Knower, you are absorbed in the space of your original self or soul, the Knower. Your original home.

The Knower is not understood with the mind because the Knower is before birth, Knower is after death, and Knower is in between.

The Knower is realized with your being.

This technique enlightens the mind to its own eternal, immortal self, your true home, the Knower.

When your meditation is over, take your own time and watch as your mind and energy begin to come to the fore. You will carry forward the space of the Knower into your daily activities, and you will see that your mind will start to think much, much better.

Amaram Hum Madhuram Hum

3. THE BHAGAVAD GITA, CHAPTER 2, VERSE 13

The Bhagavad Gita verses were written to create an atmosphere of peace, unity, and highest awareness. The practice of repeating the verses enables the mind to realize the unwavering, peaceful, established state of existence known as the Knower state of consciousness.

Here is the transliteration of the Sanskrit, the word-for-word meanings, and the translation of the verse. You can listen and meditate to me describe, discuss, and chant the verse.

dehino asmin yathā dehe kaumāram yauvanam jarā

tathā dehāntara-prāptir dhīras tatra na muhyati

Line 1: *dehino*, the soul residing in the body; *asmin*, in this; *yathā*, just as; *dehe*, in the body; *kaumāram*, childhood; *yauvanam*, youth; *jarā*, old age.

Line 2: *tathā*, even so; *dehāntara-prāptir*, acquisition of another body; *dhīras*, the wise one; *tatra*, about the matter; *na*, not; *muhyati*, gets deluded.

The underlying source of manifestation is the eternal Knower. While it dwells in the body, it witnesses childhood, youth, old age, and death and then assumes another body form. The changes happen on the level of the body form while the Knower remains forever and unchanging. The one who knows this is wise.

Shelley Astrof is a Doctor of Meditation and Peace Pioneer with extensive experience in education (M.Ed.). She holds a Certificate of Advanced Studies in Yog Science, Vedant Philosophy, and the Theory and Practice of Meditation. She is the author of *The Knower Curriculum: Teach Meditation to Children with Timeless Tales, Timeless Tales: Stories from The Knower Curriculum,* and contributed the chapter *Simple Meditation: Quiet the Mind and Heal the Body* to *The Ultimate Guide to Self-Healing Techniques.* With four decades in association with a Meditation Master in the Himalayas of India, she offers a unique perspective on meditation. As an expert meditation teacher, she will help you see beyond your visible world. As you close your eyes in meditation, you open your inner eye to your eternal true nature, your inner guidance that grounds you in your own joy and well-being, the Knower of who you really are.

Website: knower.ca/

Facebook: facebook.com/KnowerMeditation

facebook.com/shelleyastrof

Instagram: instagram.com/knowermeditation

YouTube Channel: knower.ca/youtube

CHAPTER 10

A SOLDIER'S BURIAL IN ARLINGTON NATIONAL CEMETERY

A CAREGIVER'S GUIDE AND PERSONAL STORY

Lisa A. Newton, M.Ed.

MY STORY

Memorial Day 2021. It is the first Memorial Day since my father's death. Our family is preparing for his funeral, which means we have been waiting a year in a grieving limbo, the standard wait time to bury a soldier at Arlington National Cemetery. This is not due to Covid-19, but due to the long and steady loss of lives to wars, official and unofficial, to the steady increase of deaths by illness, mental and physical, of our nations' multi-generational military soldiers. And so, my family has waited for June 1st, the first day I can expect a phone call from Arlington to set the date for my father's funeral. Whether the family religious practices align with such a delay or not, body burials are no longer accepted. Only cremated bodies are accepted for burials. Fortunately, my father's wishes were cremation and inurnment in the Columbarium or Niche Wall. The Columbarium is located at the edge of the cemetery near the Pentagon. When my mother dies, she will be cremated and join my father in the same wall niche. This has always been my parents' plan.

My father deteriorated over decades from a traumatic brain injury and cancer, but even with all the time to prepare for his death, it still came as a shock because of Covid-19. My family did our best to champion my father's life to be as full and as safe as possible for him and the rest of the world. He was an intelligent and well-trained Vietnam combat soldier with PTSD (post-traumatic stress disorder) and a TBI (traumatic brain injury). He was skilled and dangerous. We knew that he would never want to cause harm to others, so we waited as long as possible to take his gun permit, driver's license, and his legal sovereignty. This meant my mother had to dedicate her life to his care. My father spent the last thirty years of his life embedded in his church-focused life and volunteering. He focused on his grandchildren and attended every event he could.

When the Covid-19 isolation period hit, my father's mental and physical health required him to be in fully supervised nursing care away from my mother. My mother, brother, and I were no longer able to interact with my father in person. Due to his mental and physical decline, he could not utilize Facetime or Zoom to communicate with us remotely. As his good days were few-and-far-between, my mother would stand at his bedroom window and talk with him through the glass. For five years, she had visited him daily in his assisted living. She supplemented his care with her own time and efforts and fought with everything she had to keep him alive. Covid-19 was the only thing that could separate my father from his family. The rules around Covid-19 were cruel to the elderly and infirm. My father's health rapidly declined, and we could not see him. I would follow his activities and nutritional data on the care facility's website, only to learn my father was skipping meals to sleep or refusing snacks. I sent protein drinks and pudding to him through Amazon. The Covid-19 lockdown began in March 2020, and on June 9th, 2020, he was moved into hospice, where the rules allowed us to physically see him. My mother and I arrived together and found my father fifty-five pounds lighter than the last day we saw him. He had no fat nor muscle tone on his face, neck, arms, and legs, but his torso was engorged with blood from the cancer tumors rupturing. He was a skeleton of flesh and bones trying to lift a spoon of oatmeal with raisins to his mouth. He was so weak that I fed him a few bites and lifted his water straw to his mouth to drink as my mother talked to the nurse in the hallway. He looked at me and said, "Where have you been?"

When I was fifteen years old, my father received his last orders. As a career U.S. Army officer, he was proud of his station in the Office of the Surgeon General at the Pentagon. One of the first family ventures was to Arlington National Cemetery to see the Tomb of the Unknown Soldier at the changing of the Old Guard. It was a thick, humid August day. The sun was high in the sky, and the heat seemed equally oppressive from above as the marble steps and observation platform beneath my feet. I watched as the Old Guard soldiers' highly choreographed, bayonetted riffled ritual in utter silence, a knot in my stomach, and tears swelling in my eyes. What I experienced came from a common knowledge and emotional reaction of military children; it threads us silently together: soldiers die. The grand tomb and immaculate soldier guards felt fitting. It all felt honorable. I witnessed a ritual truly respectful to the unknown soldiers interred, and to all unrecovered soldiers this tomb symbolized. I was so deeply moved by that first visit that I returned alone many times over the years to watch the guards and took comfort that they were there at the cemetery to ensure the sacred resting place space. During my teen years, my family also attended the Easter Sunrise Services in the grand marble amphitheater. Both the tomb and the amphitheater are places where I felt a positive, protective spirit.

"Your father and I will be buried in the Columbarium here." My mother stated with a smile. "Let's go look at it after we go see JFK."

It was the first time I had even thought about my parents' death, and it was a shock to my teenage brain when I saw the industrial-looking structure of the Columbarium. To me, it looked like endless rows of light gray cement bowling lockers stacked too high to retrieve your ball safely. I reached out and touched one. It was cool to the touch. I ran my finger over the identification letter and numbers in the upper corner. I wondered which one was theirs? I avoided that part of the cemetery until recently.

Over the next forty years, my parents would often take day trips to Arlington to walk the grounds before shopping at the Fort Meyer's Exchange or PX. I, too, was drawn to the cemetery. It was a ritual that I went back to be a part of; in the cold and rain of winters, I sat alone, mentally communing with neat rows of souls as a curious witness. I felt the strongest connection recently at my father-in-law's funeral. He was a former member of the Old Guard and was joining his wife, who was already buried in their shared plot. As we walked from the little chapel down to his graveside casket, I saw a woman having a picnic on the freshly covered ground of a grave. My eyes met hers, and she looked through me, with eyes I assumed were locked into her own memories. I thought it was wonderful that she was visiting her son in this way. After the funeral, my husband, daughter, and I walked to visit his grandparents buried two rows away and then to the Columbarium. I noticed several benches where I thought that I would come and read the Sunday newspaper or a Clancy novel as my version of a picnic visit one day. *That will be my visitation ritual*, I thought to myself as we left to join my husband's family at an Irish Pub for the after-funeral remembrance party. So, if you ever go to Arlington National Cemetery and see me reading somewhere amongst the Columbarium, please stop and say hello, and I will ask, "How are you enjoying your visit to Arlington today?"

Prior to my father's death, I began writing my father's eulogy as a process that helped me make sense of his life journey. I first wrote about all his accomplishments, medals, and life highlights. I spent a great deal of time reviewing and revising it as I helped my mother downsize to a retirement community condo. I found the picture of his first day of kindergarten. I found his National Honor Society graduation cord. I held his Purple Heart and other medals and thought about Vietnam and the source of his traumatic brain injury that slowly and progressively destroyed his grasp on reality. As I helped move him from one assisted living place to a more progressive care facility for his cancer-filled body and atrophying brain, my eulogy focus changed to his core attributes. My eulogy ebbed and flowed from thousands of words to a few sentences that summed up why he received his last recognition from Serving Our Willing Warrior (S.O.W.W.), doing what he loved best, helping others.

Before my father took a turn for the worse, he spent his time deeply involved with the local Methodist church, visited with the local fire department, the local police patrols, and most of all, he worked tirelessly and joyfully for the S.O.W.W. organization. During his years of volunteering, his health steadily declined, and these wonderful people adjusted what they asked from him so he could continue to participate. And in the end, he became a recipient of the support the S.O.W.W. offers injured soldiers recovering from severe long-term injuries. My father's smiling face fills a memorial frame in the physical therapy basement of the grand house on the S.O.W.W. property for all wounded soldiers and their families to see and know that someone just like them helped build this beautiful place for them to heal together. I love S.O.W.W. and invite you to learn more about them and their mission to help military families recover from severe military injuries.

The process of writing a eulogy is a healing process for the living. Although sometimes I think the Vikings had it right, throw all the treasured, worldly items on top of the dead body and set it all ablaze to rejoin the elements of the earth. I have fantasized about building a fire pit and burning everything in a giant release of complicated pain. My father was so far from being perfect. His life was sprinkled densely with horrific mistakes that at times shadowed his accomplishments as a husband, father, and soldier. That is honestly said about any human being, is it not?

The year it took to schedule the funeral has provided another form of unexpected healing called reflection. Our entire family has experienced the power that time grants to the healing process. My father's treasures have been sorted and shared. The legal "this and that" has long been settled and accepted by all. The relationships that were dependent on my father being alive have faded away. And my eulogy has come down to this, "Thank you for joining us today as we say our final goodbyes to my dad, also known as, Pepaw, Harve, John, and Johnny. No matter which name or phase of his life you knew him in, he had these steady qualities about him: first, he only wanted to be of helpful service; second, he respected nature by planting trees, picking up trash from waterways, and hunting with a bow when he was on the top of his hunting game; and third, he was a fantastic grandfather. Dad, I thought it was really great that you chose your last meal to be oatmeal and your last words to be a claim that Mom was your wife. Now we place your ashes in Arlington National Cemetery with all the other soldiers. Your journey is over." My simple eulogy brings me comfort. While I watch others go through their mourning process for my father, I can only suggest that they utilize a writing process to help them navigate the difficulties that lead to emotional healing.

A GUIDE TO BURYING A SOLDIER IN ARLINGTON NATIONAL CEMETERY

From my experience, I offer these tips for burying a soldier at Arlington National Cemetery:

1. Use a hospice program or move your soldier to a hospice center that specifically has experience with Arlington National Cemetery. Use a funeral service provider who has experience with cremation for soldiers being buried at Arlington National Cemetery.

2. If your soldier is in a VA hospital or medical facility, they will assist your family seamlessly through the process of applying and arranging the burial in Arlington National Cemetery.

3. Former President Obama has issued a letter of gratitude to all Vietnam soldiers on their death beds. Former President Trump has issued a letter of gratitude for all soldiers. It is a ceremony offered at the bedside in knowledgeable hospice programs and at VA hospitals. This ceremony is an honorable way to acknowledge that the soldier's battle to survive is over, and the Commander and Chief is acknowledging their sacrifices on behalf of the nation. It is hard for caregivers because it requires them to also surrender the fight. I highly suggest all families accept this ceremony and keep the letters and pins to place with the funeral flag box, behind the memory photograph, or album.

4. The hospice will issue a death certificate. They will ask the family specific questions, and it is important to respond accurately. One question is about exposure to "Agent Orange." The other is about injury during active combat. There is one chance to answer questions accurately, and failure to do so could result in the inability for spouses to collect after-death benefits.

5. As soon as your soldier arrives in hospice services, your family will be asked to select a funeral home. The first question you should ask to determine your answer is, "Which one will perform a certified 100% cremation of the remains and issue a cremation certificate with cremation identification number annotated on the cremation certificate?" This is essential because you must have a cremation certificate that includes the name of the deceased, date of cremation,

name of crematory, signature or electronic stamp, and cremation tag number. If any of these do not happen, then your soldier will not be buried at Arlington National Cemetery.

6. During the physical dying process, the person is aware of their surroundings and the general vibe of the atmosphere. They can hear you and experience you and the others in the room. Their mind and soul are connecting with the process of leaving the earthly body and ending their physical, earthly journey. Use this time wisely and give gifts to them, like comfort, favorite songs, visits from family, smells, laughter, tales from good times, and be sure to tell them that they have done all they can do in this lifetime. When my father was dying, I stayed in the room on the chair that converted to a bed. On the second night, a nurse asked me if I had eaten, and I realized I had not. If there is someone or a rotation of people, who can stay round the clock, that is best. I kept visual over my father's pain levels and anxiety levels; it was my last act of kindness I could offer him. It also helped me get through the grieving process better.

7. Once the funeral home has collected the body, you will make the first call to Arlington National Cemetery at 1-877-907-8585 and email all required documents to arlingtoncemetery.isb@mail.mil for burial at Arlington. The required documents will take a great deal of effort and may cause great stress for family members to gather. If this becomes an issue, it is recommended that the family seek help. My family had to seek an advocate when my father's honorable discharge papers were questioned. The advocate helped us get the discharge papers reissued, along with other documents that needed to be official copies. I recommend first calling the Veterans Affairs to seek accurate and free directions for all paperwork requirements at MyVA411 at 1-800-698-2411. Required documents include the following: An official copy of birth certificate, official copy of marriage license if applicable, DD2014 or equivalent service documentation showing honorable discharge and active duty service, official death certificate, official cremation certificate, and succession document for the person authorized to direct disposition (PADD) to act on behalf of the primary next of kin (PNOK).

THE TOOL

A routine ritual I performed to keep myself from being overwhelmed by the needs of my father's care was to take sacred showers. A sacred shower is a form of release meditation that releases stress and is an act of self-care. Scared bathing is an ancient practice that spans world cultures and religions.

Step one, announce your sacred shower time and secure that nothing will interfere. Turn off your phone, tell everyone that you will be unreachable for one hour, lock the door to your house, lock the door to your bedroom, lock the door to your bathroom.

Step two, prepare your bathroom and shower. Turn off the electricity and light the room with candles. Fill your bathroom with your favorite refreshing and calming scents using essential oils, soaps, and hair cleaning products.

Step three, shower without reservation. Deny yourself nothing; grant yourself permission for everything. I suggest wearing your favorite jewelry, deep conditioning your hair, using as much hot water as you like, using a giant towel, a glass of wine, and singing at full volume if you are so inclined.

Step four, establish a sacred ritual shower chant. You can use mine or create one that will flow from your intentions freely. "Water, wash the stress and worries from my body as you wash the dirt from my skin." Chanting while you care for yourself will fill the wellspring that lives in the base chakra. Visually create your sacred ritual chant with metaphysical messages by placing stones from each chakra level in your bathroom and bring agates into your shower.

Step five, dry and secure. After you have showered and dried your body, drink a glass of water, and utilize your renewed state by engaging in further meditation or taking a well-deserved nap. Repeat as desired.

Lisa A. Newton, M.Ed. is a lifelong special education and English as a second language educator. She has developed three virtual language arts curriculums and currently teaches in a public school system. She uses her gifts as an intuitive and empath to fulfill her calling as a teacher. She believes that all people have gifts and spiritual powers that they just need to learn how to tap into them, and the key is the use of positive affirmations, learning from elders, and meditation journeying.

Also known as The Intuitive Eye Jewelry Maker, she is the owner of Earth Affirmations. She selects her stones and crystals by feeling the vibrations. She creates her metaphysical jewelry while in a meditative state and uses fine sterling silver to maximize the energetic connectivity. Her work is available at The Black Crow Art Gallery in Sandwich, Massachusetts

Black Crow Gallery | Local Art & Funky Finds
https://blackcrowartgallery.wordpress.com/

Facebook https://www.facebook.com/EarthAffirmationsLisa/

Etsy https://www.etsy.com/shop/EarthAffirmations

EarthAffirmations.com http://earthaffirmations.com/

RESOURCES

Arlington National Cemetery Eligibility Resource:

https://www.arlingtoncemetery.mil/funerals/scheduling-a-funeral/establishing-eligibility

Tomb of the Unknown Solider:

https://www.youtube.com/watch?v=vdmWB4DxdMw

Serving Our Willing Warriors:

Facebook Link: https://www.facebook.com/WillingWarriors/

CHAPTER 11

CONSCIOUS DYING

STAYING PRESENT, ALIGNED, AND CONNECTED TOGETHER

Kathy Guidi

MY STORY

I sat sobbing while trying to listen to the hospice social worker explain what to expect. "The body will shut down slowly, his food intake will dissipate, he'll begin to have difficulty swallowing, and he'll sleep more." "We know," she said, "that hearing is the last sense to go." When I exclaimed, "But he's deaf!" she replied, "Don't worry, he will hear you." The tears flowed, and I said I was just so sad. "Of course you are," she commented, "You're losing the first man you ever loved."

My parents had just celebrated their fiftieth wedding anniversary in May, and we traveled from New Zealand to Florida to visit and celebrate with them. I'd only returned home when a few weeks later, I received a call from my mom.

"Dad's not feeling too well, and there's something unusual on his x-ray. They think it's cancer."

We waited anxiously over the next weeks while Dad had further tests. As I braced myself to face one of my biggest fears, my world tunneled and narrowed to the one point of news I didn't want to hear: *Dad has metastasized cancer and has been given six to nine months to live.* So began the grief.

I bought myself a one-way ticket back to Florida, and I said goodbye to my husband, knowing I would not see him until after my father died. I was scared, very scared. I'd never been a witness or close to someone dying, and I had no idea how I would keep it together for myself, for my parents, and most importantly, for my father.

As I put my life in order and got my bags packed, the first of many angels appeared in the form of two friends who had been through this before. Introducing me to Elizabeth Kubler-Ross' five stages of dying as well as sharing their personal stories of nursing loved ones through death, they told me, "You got this."

Shortly after arriving in Florida from forty hours of travel, a meeting was convened with the hospice team, including a nurse, a social worker, and a sign language interpreter. We exchanged pleasantries, and they asked Dad some general questions. They explained about the services Hospice provides. And then they dropped the bomb that made the unreal real. "Where do you want to die?" the social worker asked. "At home," my father signed. My mom's eyes widened, and my heartbeat raced. I held back my tears and wondered how we would have the strength to care for him. "No problem," they said. "We can make you comfortable at home for as long as possible."

Those first weeks were hard. My mom and I had different opinions about what Dad should do. We spoke to numerous doctors who offered new techniques to prolong his life but would be grueling for an 81-year-old man to endure. I wanted to feed him healthy food, Mom wanted him to try one of the treatments, and he wanted neither. Dad was taking charge of how he wanted it to go, and we needed to get on board quickly.

Soon a turning point occurred for both Dad and me. Dad was sleeping in his room with the door slightly ajar, and as I walked by, I heard noises. As I came closer, I realized he was crying. In fact, he was sobbing, and this lasted for several hours. I had never seen my dad cry, and he didn't know I could hear him. And I believe this was the moment when he accepted that he was soon to die and would not make it to see the birth of his second grandchild. In that moment, I finally realized my job was to be present to what was happening and to do the best I could to help him cross over with as much love, grace, and wisdom as possible. We needed to be *his* support team and put *his* desires and wishes above our own.

He became quieter after that day and didn't have much to say, nor did he want to see many people. His daytime naps stretched to hours, and I often passed the time sitting by his bedside meditating or chanting. One afternoon as I was doing the latter, his fingers started moving along to my chants. He was hearing me.

I had *my* support team too. A few close friends made themselves available to me at all times. I would call them and offload my grief and sorrow and process the hardships of the day. Their compassion and love formed an energetic cocoon around my tender soul. The local library became a quiet haven where I could escape into myself and read about the death and dying process and what was to come.

I made time for self-care practices through the long, purgatory-like, hot Floridian summer days where one could see the steam rising from the asphalt. Evening bike rides, yoga classes, swims, and walks in nature were all salves to my breaking heart. I started going to an art therapy class and making collages as a way to tend and process my grief. I made one collage to honor my parents: it was colorful, rich with symbolism, and alive. I presented it to them, and we proudly displayed it on the living room mantle. This collage would end up being a visual anchor point throughout Dad's dying process.

My pregnant sister, her husband, and their two-year-old daughter arrived in August to have a family summer gathering while Dad was still well. My niece and my father enjoyed a special bond and could communicate deeply without speaking words. In this first week, we enjoyed family meals together, walks down memory lane, and he watched my niece and I paint together. He perked up when my niece would snuggle next to him and sign, "I love you, Papa." We got Dad's legal papers in order, and we spoke about his burial wishes. I asked if he wanted to reconnect with his brothers from whom he'd been estranged for decades, to which he replied no. These were difficult conversations for our family to delve into, but I knew they were important to have.

Within a week, Dad took a turn for the worse, and we began more intense care. We brought in a hospital bed and moved him from the bedroom to the living room, where he could stay central to the family. The nurses talked us through any questions or concerns we had and showed us how to dispense morphine to alleviate his increasing pain. He started to lose control and strength of his arms and hands, which meant he could not sign to us. My sister and I were on high alert for any cues from him—any slight movements of hands, eyes, or noises. Often he could only offer a tilt of his head to answer our yes or no questions. One afternoon Dad woke from a nap with glazed eyes and asked for Mom. I wasn't sure if he was asking for our mother or seeing his deceased mother. After gently questioning him, I determined it was the latter—he was getting glimpses of the other side. I relayed my conversation to the nurse, and she recommended he be transferred to the hospice wing of the local hospital, where he could have more attendant care. He was getting close, and we were too weary and scared to keep him home any longer.

Sister Dorothy, a family friend and angel to our family, suggested Dad and we meet the hospital priest who visited the ward daily. Dad was not a practicing Catholic, and we were a bit hesitant, but we agreed. Father Gabriel, an avatar of Jesus, arrived with boisterous joy and vitality. He took in the scene of our room: my niece's artwork taped on the walls, my collage and framed family photos displayed on the window sill, a few balloons hanging in the air. He walked to the collage, picked it up, and made me tell him all about it. "Yes, this is good."

Dad was propped in his bed, and though he was too weak to sign, his eyes tracked everyone and were alert to what was going on around him. Father Gabriel chatted with him using basic hand gestures and translating through us. Within fifteen minutes, he and Dad formed a powerful connection. Father Gabriel knew how to do one sign, "I love you," and he wove his hand through the air smiling at him. Tears leaked out of Dad's eyes.

This final week of Dad's life was an intense rollercoaster through the duality of grief and joy, pain and love, and an exercise in faith and courage to stay present and aligned to the process of dying. We had a sign language interpreter assigned to us each day; one of the family was there all the time; I spent my nights in the room sleeping by his side, often holding his hand. My niece came to visit and kept us in awe with her ability to remain present to the entire situation, never questioning or being afraid by her papa's visual decline. She brought joy to many on the ward.

Father Gabriel came twice a day, always with a smile. He asked Dad, via the interpreter, a series of questions to determine where Dad was in his emotional process. *Any regrets? Any reconciliations needed? Any concerns?* All to which my dad responded in the negative. He asked my mom and dad what their favorite drinks were. "Cappucino!" Mom exclaimed.

Father Gabriel routinely pulled me aside during this week and offered insights and clues on what I should do. I would absorb what he said and then relay the information to my sister, and we would figure out how to deliver the messages to Dad during moments of his lucidity. "You need to tell your dad his legacy. You need to tell him that you will all look out and always be there for your mother. You need to tell him that it is okay to go. You need to give him space to die."

The doctors couldn't tell us how much longer Dad would live, so we decided it would be best if my brother-in-law took my niece back home to California. Mom, my sister, and I would then be able to give all our attention to Dad. On the day they were due to fly away, in a pre-dawn hour, Dad came out of a semi-comatose state and signed to my mom and me, "I know I'm going to die. I know I'm going to die, and I'm not afraid." He then asked to see his granddaughter, not knowing she was due to leave later that day. I rang my sister and told her to bring my niece to the hospital one more time.

Mid-morning, right after the doctors made their rounds, my sister, brother-in-law, and niece came strolling into the room. Father Gabriel arrived shortly after that with two cappuccinos in his hands. Dad was unusually awake and alert, and his eyes widened when he smelled the coffee. "Can I have that?" He'd barely been able to take in applesauce the past few days yet eagerly reached for the cappuccino and began delightfully taking in its aroma and flavor while taking small sips. My niece was full of energy and brought her papa a new painting which he studied and then directed us to hang on the wall. For a short while, the room came alive. Everyone was talking and smiling. The nurses were even surprised at this burst of energy from Dad. Finally, time for my niece to leave, she nonchalantly waved and signed, "Bye-bye Papa, I love you." Dad said goodbye with the utmost grace and composure that was bittersweet to witness. The celebration lasted about an hour longer, and then Dad grew tired and gently closed his eyes and receded back into a semi-comatose state.

The three of us held vigil by his side, talking aloud and stroking his hand. He would periodically open his eyes and have a moment of awareness of us by his bedside. His last form of communication was his request for a kiss—he puckered his lips ever so slightly, and we gave him what he wanted.

Another day passed, and we knew it was just a matter of time. Heeding Father Gabriel's advice, we all left one morning to have a shower at home. We joyfully spoke aloud, "Dad, we're leaving you alone for a little while. We love you. If you need to go, now is a good time." We kissed him and walked out of the room, instructing everyone to leave him alone and not contact us. We would be back in a few hours.

He died fifteen minutes later. It had only been two months since his diagnosis and a little more than one month since my arrival. He did it his way, on his own terms, in his own time, peacefully and consciously. To be witness to the sacredness of dying was the greatest gift my father gave me.

THE TOOL

Creating a P.A.C.T.: Presence, Alignment, and Connection Together

I offer this tool with the acronym of P.A.C.T. to help the caregiver navigate a journey through death with consciousness and awareness. These are concise concepts that take the strength of mind and heart to employ. Doing so will allow for a great gift to be realized: the gift of love and sacred witnessing.

Presence: *Follow* the dying person's moods, desires, and expressions and tune into what they are saying. Put your thoughts and desires aside about how you want them to die and listen acutely to what they say. Be open to the mystery of the inexplicable and the miracles of the deathing process. Be prepared to change everything you ever knew and allow the dying person to die how they want.

Alignment: These are the *practical* things you can do. Breathe, meditate, pray. Surround yourself with a support team for YOU: friends, other family, counselors, or clergy. Your support team is there to be present for you.

Ensure you take time for self-care practices: walks, yoga, going to the gym, exercising, receiving a massage, rest. Whatever it is you do to stay grounded is paramount to continue regularly. You need to take care of yourself so that you can take care of the dying.

Connection Together: Connection is *co-created*. When you are present and aligned, you can then connect together, heart-to-heart, soul-to-soul. If the dying person is receptive, you can bring up potentially difficult questions: Where do they want to die? What are their thoughts about dying? Are there any amends they wish to make? Do they need to reconnect to anyone from their past? Do they have any regrets? Any unfinished business? Are they worried about anyone they're leaving behind? What are their burial and post-mortem memorial wishes? Are they happy with their legacy? Do you need to tell them their legacy? What did their life mean to you? How have they impacted your life? What were the gifts they gave you?

Talk openly about your feelings. This may be difficult to do, especially if you did not enjoy a close relationship with the person, but opening your heart to this sacred last rite of passage will leave you, the living, without any regrets.

And lastly, give them space to die. We might think we're showing love and providing comfort by keeping vigil around the clock, but some people will not die in front of their family. Hospice observations indicate many men and some women prefer to die alone. Keeping vigil is a beautiful thing, but take a moment to leave the room, if even for fifteen minutes.

What formed through my journey with Dad was a sacred P.A.C.T. Through remaining present and aligned, I was able to stay connected to him and instinctively know, with the right guidance, how to help him die. I hope this P.A.C.T. tool offers insight, confidence, and inspiration that you too can aid another to die consciously and at peace.

Kathy Guidi is co-creator and kaitiaki (steward) of Birdsong Retreat & Sanctuary, a place for wellness and spiritual healing. She is a certified Shamanic Breathwork facilitator and Ordained Minister (through Venus Rising Association for Transformation), a Reiki Master, a retreat facilitator, caterer of plant-based nourishing kai (food), an earth honoring ritualist and apprentice in the Pachakuti Mesa Tradition of Peru, a death-positive advocate, and a spiritual mentor. She holds both bachelor's and master's degrees in business and finance.

She is an all-around WOW-girl (ways of wellness) seeking to optimize body, mind, and spirit. She left a well-paying corporate and urban lifestyle in San Francisco for greener pastures in rural New Zealand, where she has been living on a ten-acre slice of paradise with her husband since 2006. In the early days, the sanctuary was for their own healing, then slowly became a place for friends and travelers to find respite. Since building their Temple of Venus, they have been hosting and facilitating small boutique transformational wellness events focusing on shamanism and shamanic practices.

She is passionate about earth stewardship, sacred relationship/ayni with all things and beings, and helping people with their journeys towards wholeness. In this second phase of life, her passion centers around personal development, understanding the psyche, healing our internal wounds, and becoming conscious, heart-centered humans.

You can find her dispensing wisdom to friends and guests from the garden, from the kitchen, or from the comforts of their cozy couches. She offers group shamanic breathwork sessions at retreats and co-facilitates quarterly women's gatherings: www.birdsongretreat.nz. She is currently working on her doctorate in psycho-spiritual studies with Venus Rising University and is soon to launch her personal website www.kathyguidi.com.

Further resources and information on conscious dying can be found at www.birdsongretreat.nz/sacred-death/.

CHAPTER 12

HOW YOGA CHANGED MY LIFE

A STORY OF YOGA APPLIED TO LIFE AND DEATH

Jill Mollenhauer, 500hr E-RYT, Yoga Therapist

MY STORY

Take a deep breath in and let it go. Take another one and another. This is what we call in yoga our "life force." My favorite quote is: *If you can breathe, you can do yoga.* There are so many misconceptions about the practice of yoga, and I bought into them all at first. You see, yoga truly has changed my life; what's more, it continues to do so in so many ways every day.

My story is not unique or unusual—no earth-shattering experiences leading me to this practice. I started when someone said I should give it a try while pregnant with my first child. I did feel great afterward because of the sense of connection I felt with myself and my baby. Fast forward to a busy life of a new baby, job, and then a huge move to a different state and a huge feeling of disconnect. Again, someone says, "you should try yoga." This time, it took, and I have never looked back. In the early 2000s, I took my first yoga teacher training and started teaching right after I graduated.

Scared to death, I fell in love and honestly have been teaching ever since. Fast forward two years: I took my first yin yoga teacher training, and that's when a true love affair began. The connection of mind, body, breath, and spirit took hold. I started to understand the path of yoga and how deep and far it went. The path is a guide to life, how we live it, and how deeply we love ourselves and one another.

Take another deep breath in, and now hold it in for just a moment, then let it go and hold it out for another moment. Do that a couple more times, please. It feels good, doesn't it?

Over the past several years, many certifications, thousands of hours studying and teaching, leading my own training, this is what I know for sure: I am more humble, kinder, more compassionate, not as quick to judge, and more likely to give you a hug. I will never stop learning, and I will never tire of this practice.

I have, like you, experienced great joy, love, sorrow, and pain in my life. Because of this practice, I have transformed and continue to do so. I can honestly say that without this practice, my perspective would not be as it is today. Even through the pain we all experience, yoga offers the perspective that not only "this too shall pass," but we must live in the pain and not try to pass by it. People say that the only thing that's constant in life is change, but do we really think about it or just say it? I wonder about that.

I have embarked on a new venture in this part of my life, and it just seems natural. Let me explain the bridge between yoga and this new calling. In yoga, savasana, or corpse pose, is said to be the most challenging of all postures. We are supposed to be still and rest, which is hard enough, but we must also contemplate our own death. To feel what that will be like one day, imagine what it will be like to not be here. Enter in End-of-Life Doula. I mentioned to a friend one day that I really wanted to help people transition from this life to whatever comes next. It is often overlooked or scary, lonely, or all of the above. She suggested I look into it. As fate would have it, I found an introductory seminar, and that was it. You see, in my own practice, I've been thinking about my own passing, which has made me appreciate my life even more every day. I want to honor death as a part of life, not just an ending. I have started doing this for others, and I know I'm receiving far more than I give.

Such is the circle of life, and what a life it is! Take another deep breath, please. Do that as many times as you possibly can because each breath is a gift. Take in a moment, a laugh at something really funny, a touching moment that pulls at your heartstrings. These moments will never come again. I'm reminded of sending my daughter to grad school two states away. She is my light and my joy and must go spread her wings. The pain of letting her go was more than I thought I could bear, but it was supposed to happen, right? The moment I hugged her goodbye and held her tight, not wanting to let go, I took it in, breathed it in. We don't just breathe in the joy, but also the pain because it too shall pass. Let us move onto the tools we can use throughout our lives that make every part of it that much sweeter.

THE TOOLS

Breath, movement, stillness…the end. I'm kidding, sort of, but that's the idea. Can we talk about our diaphragm for a moment? You see, most of our lives, we do what's called "reverse breathing." As babies and children, we breathe deep, but around puberty, we start to shorten our breath, and it moves up higher in the chest. We puff our chest out and suck our tummy in, thinking this is a deep breath, and then we do this from that point on usually. Put your hand on your tummy, please. Now take a deep breath in and see if you can start your breath at your hand and feel it rise to your ribcage and then into your chest. As you exhale, see if you can relax the tummy, then ribs, then your chest. To take a deep breath is to practice yoga. The yoga postures or asanas are of great use in transforming our energy. What I'm about to say may blow your mind, but our spine only has five movements; five. Yoga moves our spine in all these ways; backward bending, forward folds, side stretches, twists, and sitting with what is called a neutral spine. Side note and great news: We can do all of this in a chair and even lying down! Yoga is accessible to everybody. What's more, there are so many lessons to be learned from this practice, lessons on how we live and, yes, how we die. It's a path to travel both on and off our mats.

Let's move our spine now. You can either sit in a chair or be on your hands and knees. If you are on the floor, gently drop your tummy towards the floor as you lift the crown of your head and tailbone to the ceiling. If you are sitting, gently press your chest forward, arching your spine, and ease your head back. This is cow pose or a backbend. Now we will reverse this. Round your spine toward the ceiling or the back of your chair and gently tuck your chin to your chest, forward folding the spine; this is cat pose. Let's connect the breath here. Inhale as you backbend and exhale as you forward fold, and repeat. You can add a gentle stretch to the side as well as a twist here. The idea is to gently move your spine and connect with your breath. This is incredible for your spine and all the energy in your body. Simple, yet we rarely do this. Yes, we are lines of energy that become stuck and tight over time, causing all sorts of issues. Move your spine every day, and you will feel the difference both physically as well as energetically.

One of the best postures for our overall health is called "legs up the wall." Ease your hips to a wall, lay down, and put your legs up the wall. If your low back lifts off the floor, place a blanket under your hips for support. If the floor is not the place for you, you can sit in a chair and put your legs on another chair. This is wonderful for relaxing your legs, hips, and low back. Stay here and breathe deeply for as long as you'd like. Another beautiful posture is called "supported butterfly." There are many ways to support yourself in this position. You can place a bolster or a rolled-up towel on the floor vertically or horizontally along your spine and then put your feet together and let your knees ease apart. Let your arms spread out away from your sides to open up your chest as well as your heart. If it's too much of a stretch on the inner thighs, you can place towels or blocks at your outer thighs for support. Stay here and connect with your breath for as long as you'd like, never moving towards discomfort or pain. In this posture, we open up the front line of energy in our body and connect with our heart. Feelings of vulnerability, love, and joy often come up here. Embrace them, sit with them, and notice what comes up for you. Ultimately yoga means to connect or to "yoke" mind, body, and breath. The lessons we can learn here are many. How do we live, love, and let go? We inhale and let it go as we exhale, not knowing if we get the gift of another breath.

We must celebrate our transition out of this life as we celebrate coming in. The life we live, the path we take, and how we leave are equally important. Practice makes practice, not perfect. I think of this every time I practice yoga. I am not trying to perfect my postures, my breath, or my body. I am trying to connect with myself, so I connect with others in a more profound way. As we take those deep breaths in our practice and move our energy, we become more aware of how we are with those around us. We are here to love and to be loved. As we move our life force, we open up to others in a more profound way. We give more, share more, and feel more, which can be scary and quite liberating!

I hope you open your heart and soul to this practice breath by breath. Breathe deeper every chance you get. You can do it right now, as you drive, walk your dog, or do the dishes. If you can breathe, you can do yoga. So it's not about being on a yoga mat or in a yoga class, even. Sit for a moment, close your eyes, and take a deep breath in and let it go.

If you are interested in the path of yoga, I will include the path here. First, there are the Yamas: Ahimsa (non-violence), Satya (truthfulness), Asteya (non-stealing), Brahmacharya (right use of energy), Aparigraha (non-greed.) Next are the Niyamas: Saucha (cleanliness), Santosha (contentment), Tapas (discipline or burning desire), Svadhyaya (self-study), Isvarapranidahana (surrender.) Those are the first two. The third limb are the Asana or postures, followed by Pranayama, the breath. The fifth limb is Pratyahara, withdrawal of the sense. The sixth is Dharana, or concentration. The seventh is Dhyana, or meditation. And last but not least is Samadhi, or pure contemplation.

Wow, that is a lot! A lifetime of discovery if you are willing to learn. A wonderful teacher once said that our lesson is our yoga practice, but true yoga is what happens outside of that, how we interact with ourselves and others in our daily lives. Once again, I will say that practice makes practice. It is my humble opinion that we're not here to perfect anything. We are here to love, learn, share, and connect with ourselves and others. Take it all in, every moment, because that moment is all we have. I will end my chapter with a quote:

Zen pretty much comes down to three things—everything changes; everything is connected; pay attention.

~Jane Hirshfield

Jill Mollenhauer was born in Iowa but now calls Colorado her home. She has two amazing children who are now launched out into the world, and two rescue dogs to spoil because they deserve it. She has been a practicing Esthetician for the past 34 years and still loves taking care of people's skincare needs. Over 20 years ago, she was introduced to yoga with her first pregnancy, but the practice really took hold in the early 2000s and then her first teacher training in 2008. Now, with several certifications, hours of teaching, and leading others to teach their own classes under her mat, she is now embarking on a Yoga Therapy training as well as an End-of-life Doula. Through her practice, the understanding of contemplating one's own death has become a regular practice in and of itself. Through serving others comes the understanding that it is a transformation for those leaving as well as those left behind. Her adult life has been to serve others, and perhaps becoming an author is yet another way to do just that.

For more information, visit her website at; www.jill-mollenhauer.com

CHAPTER 13

HEALING AFTER LOSS

HOW FORGIVENESS LEADS TO SELF-LOVE AND INNER PEACE

Esther Reyes

MY STORY

LOSS BEFORE DEATH

I can't pinpoint the exact evening he made his announcement. The days blended into each other when the children were little. I know the girls were younger than nine-months-old. The memory rushes at me like a tsunami. It hits me without warning.

He arrived from work, as he did so many nights before. After washing up, he requested to speak to me. Feeling the intensity of his energy, I was a little apprehensive. His approach was out of character. What happened next changed everything.

He looked at me and said, "From now on, when I come home, I don't need anything from you. I don't want to talk to you. Don't ask me questions. I won't answer them. I talk all day long, and when I come home, I want to be alone in silence. When we need to talk about the children, keep it short.

And don't worry, we're still a family." He turned and left the room, leaving me frozen under the new martial laws.

I was speechless. We were married for three years and had three babies. The rejection broke me. The bit of self-worth I had oozed out of me like squeezed toothpaste from a tube. *How can he not want to talk to me? I spent all day long with our three children. The oldest was only two. He was my lifeline to the outside world. I needed him.*

He later assured me it had nothing to do with me. He simply needed his time. I never understood why he didn't see me as his fortress after a long day. Or why he didn't want me to care for him. As his wife, that was my job by default. That's what I signed up for.

I agreed to his conditions. What choice did I have? Every day that followed, he would greet me and escape to the bedroom. When I had things to do in the bedroom, he would move to the living room. We spent the rest of our married life under these circumstances.

The one thing he didn't plan for was the children. Once he arrived, they went where he went. They were hungry for him too. They rejected his demands for isolation. It turned out, he looked forward to spending time with them. I appreciated his love for our babies. That was my excuse to deem the marriage "normal." He was a good father and loved his children.

All my energy went into portraying a picture-perfect image. The world saw a loving, elegant couple with their brilliant son and their beautiful, identical twin daughters. Our family was the poster child of a successful mixed-race marriage—a real-life love story. But the reality was sadder. We were independent contractors, each with a job to do. And there was no room for failure.

Every few months, I subjected myself to reliving his rejection. I would re-evaluate our "contract" by breaking down into tears. Through my heartache, I pleaded with him to let me be his wife. I begged to be part of his world. He would sit quietly, never meeting my eyes. Eventually walking away, leaving me drowning in my ocean of pain.

The days and weeks dissolved into months and years. I came to accept his terms and stopped pressing for a relationship beyond the children. While my desire to be a wife went unmet, and our interactions limited, our home was a loving environment. The combined love for our children had power. It made everything better, including our union.

He was diagnosed with cancer three years later. He told me in such a matter-of-fact way, it took me a moment to process what he was saying. *Now he would accept me in his life. He needs me,* I thought. There was nothing in the way of me supporting him. The children were in school full-time, and I had control of the schedule for my part-time job. I was ready to take care of him. Ready to be his wife.

But that's not what he wanted.

He said he had his brother and didn't need anything from me. He shut me out throughout the entirety of his medical journey. When he needed someone to drive him or sit with him during a procedure, he chose his brother. Even when it came to assisting him at home, he preferred the children's help to mine. I dealt with the heartache the only way I knew how, by accepting the blame for all of it. I was sure I was responsible for his rejection.

On occasion, he would inform me of his current condition. But he was quick to shut down when I started asking questions. With treatment and surgery, he went into remission and remained cancer-free for the next five years.

When cancer returned, it metastasized throughout his body. I later found out he knew he was terminally ill. It must have been hard carrying such a heavy secret for over a year. I wondered if he felt he was protecting me.

The medical professionals were not allowed to inform me of his condition. I learned he was dying when they moved him to hospice. By then, he was in and out of consciousness. That's when I realized I had lost my husband eight years earlier.

After he passed away, I continued to blame myself for things I had no control of. For the pain the children were feeling, for not being enough for him, for not knowing the truth about his condition.

The guilt, anger, and self-hatred were like a volcano erupting inside me. I resented myself for not fighting harder, for not doing more to save him. I resented him for leaving his children. I resented my family for believing I could "handle it" because I'm strong. And I resented my friends who stared with pity. As if we were too broken to ever be whole again. All this resentment fueled my discontent and hopelessness.

Time passed, and the children grew. My heart got heavier and darker. My stress was through the roof. I was a full-time educator working on a second graduate degree and raising three young children alone. My bitterness, and self-condemnation grew with every new day like a tree at the edge of a river bank."

MORE LOSS AFTER DEATH

Believing I needed to replace what I never had, I remarried. This decision blew up the family. Nothing was ever the same again. What remained was more pain and more loss.

Four years after his father passed away, my only son decided he didn't want to be part of our family. He often said my Latin heritage was holding him back. He resembles his blued-eyed, light-skinned, Slavic father. His resentment was clear whenever I met his teachers for the first time.

My son no longer appreciated, nor respected my mothering skills. He rejected any attempts for compromise. He rejected me. He was in a lot of pain. But at the time, all I saw was his rage. It was a terrible season for our family; a lot of yelling, a lot of door slamming, a lot of tears. While he was going through puberty, I was going through menopause. We were two bullet trains zooming towards each other on the same track. The collision was inevitable.

Through a series of choices he made and the court's ruling, my son got what he wanted: A caucasian mother and another family. When the decision was made, it was like a boulder rushing down a hill towards me. I could not move. I was paralyzed in my pain.

My heart was beyond broken. This pain cut deeper, colder than ice. To keep warm, I wrapped myself in the blame again. It felt like a warm knitted blanket made especially for me.

With the loss of my firstborn came the loss of a burdensome, loveless marriage, a decade-long career, and stability for my daughters.

I had no choice but to move forward. So I did. I focused on my girls and their future. I found a new town, a new high school, and packed the house. The girls finished the fall semester of ninth grade, and I relocated the family.

LIFE AFTER LOSS

A new city, no job, and a heavy broken heart.

The first day the girls left for school, I spent hours crying in the shower. Not just crying, bawling. Not knowing what else to do after the emotionally draining hydrotherapy, I prayed.

I have always prayed. I've witnessed the power of prayer. But this time was different. I was at my end. I prayed like I had nothing left to give. I prayed with all my heart, with all my soul, and with all my mind.

The crying-in-the-shower, followed by intense praying, was not a one-time thing. It became my daily therapy session. Out of these spiritual and emotional encounters, I discovered myself. It was a self I did not recognize. It was in my brokenness that I was reminded I had value. I was worthy. Worthy of forgiveness. Worthy of love. Worthy of inner peace.

I was reawakened to things I enjoyed: uninterrupted reading and writing, working out, riding my bike, learning new things. Rays of light were breaking through the darkness that surrounded me. But before I could appreciate my breakthrough, I knew I needed to heal.

I was broken into so many pieces.

I didn't know where to begin. What does a "healed" me even look like? Where is the starting line for self-healing? Determined to find it, I read books, and watched videos on how to heal oneself. I was overwhelmed with all the information on the subject. It seems everyone needs healing, and everyone else knows exactly what we need to be healed.

A recurring message of self-healing is self-love. *Love of oneself. Loving yourself. Self-love?* I needed time to consider this. It was foreign to me. In my culture, women put everyone and everything above themselves. It's in my DNA.

After raising three children and teaching underprivileged students, self-love was unimaginable. I felt a rush of guilt at the thought of putting myself before others. It was like a bucket of ice water dumped over my head.

Loving myself before everyone else, is that even allowed?

I discovered inner peace grows out of love for others and self-love. And self-love is born of forgiveness. Forgiveness of others and forgiveness of self.

To arrive at a place of peace, I needed to forgive.

Forgiveness. I never considered it.

Wait, what?

I needed to forgive everyone. Just like that? But how? I've been wearing resentment, bitterness, and self-loathing like jewels on a crown. I've worn it for so long, who would I be without it?

I never considered that forgiving others would set me free. It took several days and lots of praying to commit to forgiving. To get started, I created a list.

Forgiving the father of my children came easy. Maybe because eight years have passed since he left us. Or maybe because he was a good man who loved his children.

Next on my list, my family. Finding forgiveness for this crew was harder. *La Familia* knows how to stab with accuracy. When I finally let go and forgave them, my spirit felt lighter. It was great to release the weight.

Closer to the bottom of my list was my son. I was disturbed and embarrassed how tough it was to find forgiveness for him. He had done serious damage to the family. And to me. I felt justified carrying around that heartache. *As a mother, I had the right to hold on to whatever anger, distaste, disappointment, and regret I had towards him,* I thought.

But here's the thing...

Self-love and inner peace require *Total Forgiveness*. Not partial forgiveness; forgiving some things, but not everything. And not part-time forgiveness; forgiving some days, but not every day. You need to be all-in.

It needs to be *Total Forgiveness* for everything, every day.

With time, I was able to forgive my son completely. By forgiving him, I created a space to bless him and his family.

Last on my list was me. I needed to find a way to forgive myself. It was hard. How could I justify forgiveness after all the pain I caused and all the loss we experienced?

Self-love and inner peace seemed unattainable. Unrealistic. I had a painfully long list of "crimes." I had to forgive myself for not being enough for the father of my children, for making the horrific mistake of remarrying, and for not fighting harder for my son.

Prayer and self-examination helped me see myself as I truly am, human and flawed. I spent hours in solitude. Evaluating and reflecting on my life, my decisions, and my blessings. I soon ran out of excuses for *not* forgiving myself.

The whole process of forgiveness was just that, a process. It didn't happen in days or weeks. It took months to forgive everyone. It took longer to forgive myself.

My quest towards inner peace has empowered me and elevated my self-worth exponentially. Forgiving is freeing. Forgiving and letting go creates space for growth and healing. Self-love plays an important part in healing.

Self-love is a process.

It's an Activity of Daily Living (ADL). Your ability to apply it daily will enhance your life.

THE TOOL

The following tool will help with your journey towards self-love and inner peace.

START WITH **G.R.A.C.E.**

Start with believing you deserve love. You deserve peace. Start with valuing who you are and all you have to offer. Having grace for yourself means admitting you are imperfect. Admitting you are a work in progress. Grace means knowing you will mess up, but you still love yourself.

G: GRATITUDE

Reflect on what makes your life better. Your family, your friends, your home. Anything that gives you joy. List your blessings. If you get stuck, focus on what you have instead of what you don't have. Create a list and add it to it daily.

R: REST

This can be a tough habit to enforce if you're always on the move. It will make a big difference when you are proactive with getting rest. You'll be more focused and experience fewer emotional mood swings. When you let your body and mind rest, you'll be able to deal with stress more efficiently. Figure out what works best for you.

A: AFFIRMATIONS

Think about your thinking. Words have power, positive or negative. Be gentle with yourself. Thinking or speaking destructive words only serves to tear yourself down. The words you use to describe yourself should add value to you and celebrate your potential. When negative words come up, be ready to neutralize them with pre-determined positive words or phrases.

C: CONNECT

This can be especially hard for those who are reluctant to interact with others. But connecting is a key part of moving forward. Think of someone who can be there for you without judgment. Connect the way you want— text, call, video chat, or in-person.

E: EXERCISE

Be intentional with moving your body every day. Adopt an exercise routine. There are tons of benefits to resistance training. Great things will happen to your mood, metabolism, and libido.

Born to immigrant parents, **Esther** was determined to earn her degree to honor her family. From a young age, she loved stories. Through listening, reading, and writing, she discovered her love for words. As a child, she spent her days reading. While her friends played around her, she found herself immersed in book after book, recreating and retelling stories of her own. Unconsciously paving the way for her true passion.

As life would have it, she neglected her calling and obtained not one but two graduate degrees. One in Physical Therapy and the other in teaching English to Second Language Learners. Esther loved teaching young minds to read and write. Spreading the joy she felt throughout her childhood, while nurturing their love for learning.

Esther is actively searching for new opportunities to connect with her readers and clients. She spends her days writing to persuade, engage, and influence. Currently working as a freelance copywriter, she seeks to help freelancers and entrepreneurs grow their audience by delivering copy that converts and connects.

After years of doing the expected, Esther found the road less traveled and took a bike ride on it.

As an introvert with social skills, she enjoys a smaller circle of humans. Using the 24 hours in her day to read, write, and dance like no one is watching.

Esther is a newly, self-discovered, creative living in a small city in Virginia, US with her twin daughters and two doggies; Kayla The Warrior Princess & Leo The Lion

https://www.linkedin.com/in/esther-reyes-9a6741185/

CHAPTER 14

A SACRED CEREMONY FOR WORDS

WHEN WE HAVE TO SAY GOODBYE

Carol Dutton, Energy Medicine Specialist

MY STORY

I am sitting down to enjoy my dinner when the telephone rings. *How do telemarketers seem to know when people are eating?* I pick up the handset and hear Ron's voice. "Carol, she can't get off the sofa. She's so weak, and I don't know what to do!" Tears begin to roll down my cheeks. Conveying a calm that I'm not feeling, I ask, "How long has she been like this? Never mind, you need to call for an ambulance. I will meet you at the emergency room in an hour."

She is my beautiful Aunt Sylvia. Sylvia, my mom's eldest sister, has always been special to me. She fills the role of second mom, grandmother, and best friend, all rolled into a small but larger than life, package of encouragement and kindness. Battling breast cancer for 20-plus years, she has endured a mastectomy, radiation, and chemo, which brought her several years of remission. But no longer, the breast cancer has returned and metastasized into her bones.

Thursday, August 1, 2019, Sylvia is admitted to the hospital after receiving IVs for dehydration. Determining that she needs the physical support available in a care center, the doctor talks with her about not going back to her house. In her typical matter-of-fact voice, Sylvia replies, "No, I have too much to do yet." *That's not the answer I expected. What does she have left to do? She's 93 years old! She's too weak to do anything right now.* I ask, "Auntie, what is it you have to do?" She answers, "I need to clean my house and go fishing in Canada one more time." Stifling a giggle, I interject, "Auntie, I will clean your house for you. I would love another fishing vacation with you." I see a bit of spunk return to her eyes, but just as quickly, it fades away. She says, "You are so busy taking care of your dad and Larry. I can't ask you to help me too." "Auntie, you didn't ask. I offered. Yes, I am busy, but I have time for you." *If you would just let me help. Yes, I've overseen Dad's care for the last nine years. Yes, Larry has a muscle disease. But you also need me. Over the years, I have offered many times. You always refuse. Don't do this again. You Need Me! How will I ever convince you?* With a mischievous light sparkling in her eyes, she says, "Oh, Carol. You don't know what you're getting yourself into!" Sylvia's doctor looks at her compassionately and says, "It sounds like you have help. So now, what do you think?" Her frail ninety-eight-pound body sinks back into the bed as she surrenders to the inevitable. She whispers to us, "What is there for me to say? You can arrange for the care center."

I am so happy that he told her that. It isn't safe for her to go home. Ron isn't well. He's weak and unsteady on his feet. He can't give her the help she needs. The hospital social worker meets with us. Sylvia is happy there is a room available in the rehab unit of our local care center. *I am glad she will be staying in town. I am familiar with them because that is where Dad is living. Her brother is also in the assisted living apartments there. It will be easier for him to visit.* The hospital makes the necessary arrangements. We expect she will be transferred on Tuesday.

5:00 AM Sunday, I am jolted awake as my telephone starts ringing. Jumping out of bed, I fumble to answer the phone. Worried about Sylvia, I'm surprised it isn't the hospital calling. It is the nursing home. They tell me that Dad passed away this morning. At the 3:30 AM patient check, he was awake and twiddling his thumbs. When they did their 4:45 AM check, he had already passed. *How much more loss can I deal with right now?*

Flooded with feelings that I can't give voice to, I note them to process later. Going on autopilot, I respond, "I'll be there soon."

I call my siblings to share the unexpected news before leaving home.

My siblings and I arrive at the care center. We divide and pack up Dad's belongings as we share our fond memories of him. *I'm so thankful this goes smoothly.* This was one of the memories I add to my "Blessings and Memories" chest. This is a self-care tool I created for times like this. It contains my jottings of things that make me feel good. I read them when I need a boost of happiness.

Monday, before the meeting with the funeral home to make arrangements for Dad, I go to the hospital. I need to tell my dear Aunt Sylvia about Dad. "Auntie, Dad passed away yesterday." Sinking back into her pillow, she keeps repeating, "Oh, dear. Oh, dear. Oh, dear." *I have always shared my joys and heartaches with her. Today fits both of those. I already miss Dad so much. However, that is not the point of today's conversation.* "Auntie, it is so amazing how God works wonders for us! He knew Dad was suffering, and his quality of life was no longer the greatest. God has given me the time to help take care of you by taking Dad to heaven. He knew that you truly needed me." Tears well up in her eyes; she grabs my hand and starts praying.

The following days pass with a flurry of activities: my siblings and I planning Dad's funeral, attending to Sylvia's needs at the hospital, meeting with the social worker, worrying about Ron when he's late to hospital meetings, and asking my cousin to bring Sylvia to the funeral. So many details. *No time to process my own experience or grieve for Dad.* I silently express gratitude for the understanding of my employer and co-workers. *I have security because I can use vacation hours.*

Sylvia has an appointment with the oncologist she has seen for many years. Concluding the exam, the oncologist gently says, "Sylvia do you think we should stop your cancer treatments? You are so weak and have lost so much weight. I don't know what treatments we can even give you. You have put up a good fight for many years." Quietly, Sylvia confirms, "Yes, I guess we will stop the treatments." Tears start to run down my cheek. The doctor hands me a tissue as she takes one for herself.

It's time for setting up hospice. The hospital social worker assists us. She gives us information on the three hospice services that work in our area. *How do we decide something so important from a pamphlet? One of the names jumps out at me from when my brother-in-law, Rodney, went through this with his family. I should talk with him.* The social worker gives us time to discuss it. I call Rodney for his input; now it's time to visit with Auntie. "Auntie, Rodney was extremely pleased with how St. Croix Hospice took care of Margaret. I have never heard anything bad about them. I don't know anything about the others. They might be equally as good, but ..." Interrupting me, Sylvia states, "Let's choose the one we know about."

We have many meetings with the doctors, social worker, and hospice team before she's transferred from the hospital. I meet with the team at the care center. We get her settled into her room. *What relief! She's not in the same room that Dad was transferred to just three months ago after his fall.* The transfer wasn't too much of a physical strain on her.

The St. Croix Hospice team assesses Sylvia's needs. Along with their nursing visits, they have volunteers to visit, give massages, sing, and play music. They are very thorough, asking Sylvia what her hobbies are, what music styles she likes, what concerns she has, what they can help with, and give us pamphlets with contact information. They arrange for an incredibly soft, air-filled mattress to help cushion her fragile, pain-filled body.

Two days later, because I'm listed as Sylvia's care representative, the care center staff inform me that her companion negatively impacts their ability to give her proper care. They tell me that Ron is spending the nights in the recliner in Sylvia's room. He's eating food from Sylvia's plate. It's impossible for them to chart how much food she's eating. They are also concerned about how much nutrition he's getting since he never leaves. I'm in the uncomfortable position of having to tell him he's not allowed to sleep there. He must go home! *Ron, as her companion, has been living with her for several years. He should understand as he has been in and out of other care centers to regain his strength. Sylvia visited him but never spent the night in his room. The center offers guests meals for a small fee. Why doesn't he just buy meals so he can eat with her?* Mustering up my courage for an unpleasant exchange, I get Ron alone and tell him what the staff told me. His body stiffens with hurt. He stoically says that he will stay the evening. I tell him that for his health and Sylvia's, he must leave by 8 PM. *Once again, I can't deal with my feelings right now. I will need to process them later.*

Fortunate to have daily visits, I'm kept informed by the care center staff of any changes or concerns. The hospice team is also keeping me updated with their observations. A hospice caseworker asks how I feel about a certain situation. Quickly I reply, "It doesn't matter how I feel. It only matters what I can do to ease Sylvia's transitioning time." She responds, "I wish all my clients had this unconditional support."

A few weeks later, the nurse tells me that Sylvia is expressing a need for me. She keeps asking them, "Where's my Carol? Where's my Carol?" What she wanted was to hold my hand. That is when I realize I need to spend even more time with her.

During another conversation with Sylvia's lead hospice caseworker, she asks how I'm doing. Stammering to come up with an answer, I realize I've shut off my feelings. I've stifled my grief from Dad's death and the hurt of watching Sylvia's life decline. None of it seems real. Yet it's all too real. When I get home that day, I read some of the notes in my Blessings and Memory chest. *None of them are bringing me into a sense of happiness like they usually do. I need something more. What can I do for my self-care? A soak in the tub isn't going to do it. A spa day of pampering and massage sounds wonderful, but no time to do that. I need to dig deeper for my feelings and get them to the surface. I will be no good to Sylvia if I don't care for myself. Maybe writing will allow me to get into my feelings, both the good and the bad. I don't want to keep the negative ones. Aha! I need to create a Sacred Ceremony for Words. I will write down these negative feelings then burn the paper they are written on. And follow it with sage cleansing! That will destroy any attachment to those bad emotions.*

That's it! I start by blessing the writing process. It feels good to describe some of the frustrations and emotions I didn't realize I'd bottled up, nor how they were dragging me down. Once I feel the flowing of words stop, I again say a blessing for the emotional cleansing. I tear the paper into small pieces and burn them. With my sage bundle, I cleanse the pen I used as well as the space where I sat during my writing. I can feel and have a sense of lightness that wasn't there before this Sacred Ceremony.

Aunt Sylvia is so concerned about Ron. He's now in the hospital with an infection. He's too weak to walk independently and needs two people to assist him. He is being transferred to a rehab care center in another town. They talk on their cell phones, but she has trouble hearing as hearing aids don't seem to work with her cell phone. Ron's daughter, Connie, brings him to visit Sylvia. Their visit is bittersweet as we realize it will probably be the last time they see each other. This is another note for my Blessings and Memories chest.

Aunt Sylvia is allowing me to tell some people that she's in hospice, but not everyone. I let her call all the shots. She is in charge, and I want her to know that. She gets to decide who she wants to see and who she doesn't want to see. She has many visitors: friends, people from church, and family members.

I treasure the time I'm spending with Sylvia. We talk about so many shared memories, family stories, and how much we love each other. We also talk about some of the business things of me handling her estate, such as where her investments are located, what bank she works with, where she has a safety deposit box, etc. She tells me that she has her estate set up in a trust. One day I take her to the bank so she can go through her safety deposit box. It was a horrible experience. She is worn out by the task, lays her head in her hands, and starts to cry. Facing the finality of her life is emotionally exhausting for both of us. I recall what I told her when Uncle Doug, her husband, was in hospice 14 years ago, "Auntie, if it were up to us, we would never have to say goodbye to him. But that isn't fair to him." It is good to remember those words because I don't want to say goodbye to her. But it isn't fair for her to continue suffering because of my selfishness.

It's hard to believe she has been here for only six weeks. Today the hospice nurse tells me she's deteriorating quickly. As her strength is waning, they tell me it's time to start limiting visitors. *How can I tell her church friends to stop visiting? She loves them. They still bring her joy, especially the ones who are content to simply sit and hold her hand.* I decide there are only a few people who should be told not to visit. Sylvia is spending more time sleeping. She is often too tired to eat.

Hospice is now telling me we should tell anyone who wants to see her they should do so soon. Hospice also suggests we should be letting Sylvia know we'll be okay without her. It can help her let go of us as we are letting go of her. I will do anything in my power to help ease her mind.

Bless her brother, my Uncle Ellzy, for being firm with making sure I get some good rest. Living in the same building, he takes on the evening shift of sitting with her. They spend the evenings listening to an audio of the Bible. I'm so glad they have each other. Both of her sisters have passed away. He's her only sibling still alive.

October 5, 2019, Uncle Ellzy and I are both sitting with her. Uncle is eating his breakfast as I sit holding her elbow in my hand. Her hand is resting on my arm. I suddenly feel a jolt, like a lightning bolt, run from her elbow up to my shoulder as she takes her last breath. The room is flooded with angels carrying her away. This experience is one of the jottings I add to my Blessings and Memories chest, though I doubt I will ever forget it.

THE TOOL

Our thoughts and words carry vibrations and frequencies. The positive and happy thoughts or words are of higher frequencies. Higher frequencies serve our better good.

The negative and sad thoughts or words are of lower frequencies. For emotional and physical well-being, we should not stifle those feelings, thoughts, or words. But what is a healthy way to let them out without hurting others or ourselves?

Here are two ceremonies I created. I use them to release my feelings and raise my frequency.

- A Blessings and Memories Chest is used to store the jottings and notes that remind you of good things that have happened in your life. When you feel a need to uplift your mood and spirits, simply read some of the notes in your Blessings and Memories chest. To create your Blessings and Memories, all you need is a pen, paper, and something for storage. A lidded jar, box, can, or anything that appeals to you will work for storage.

- A Sacred Ceremony for Words is one way to get rid of your negative thoughts or words. Don't speak them aloud. Bless the pen and paper you are using. Write down your thoughts. Bless the ritual of disposing of the paper. Examples of the ritual could be burning the paper, soaking it in water, burying the paper, or even shredding it. By disposing of the negative words, you don't hold onto the lower frequencies. They are not held in a residual state when you use this Sacred Ceremony. Once you have completed this ceremony, pull out something to read from your Blessings and Memories chest, if you have one.

A free PDF download of A Sacred Ceremony for Words can be found at https://beingyouenergetically.com/sacreddeathresources/

Carol Dutton is the owner of Being You Energetically, LLC and an expert Subtle Energy Practitioner, Reiki Master, Crystal Grid Healer, and an Irigenics® Ancestral Eye Reader. As a non-denominational ordained minister, she also performs spiritual oil anointing.

Whichever modality you choose, her powerful sessions will immediately give you the unique and specific missing links to clearing the traumatic and ancestral patterns keeping you from living an extraordinary life.

While spending her working career in the corporate world, she started her journey into the holistic healing world to bring comfort to her husband, who struggles with a rare muscle disease. Seeing the relief he felt after a session, Carol decided to offer the sessions to friends and family members. With their encouragement, she started offering sessions to others.

In January 2020, her corporate job was eliminated. This was the impetus for her to seriously consider opening her own business doing the work she loves. After educating herself on being a business owner, she founded Being You Energetically, LLC in January 2021.

She lives in rural Minnesota with her husband. Her hobbies include gardening, preserving food from her garden and farmer's market, beekeeping, reading, and fishing.

She is a storyteller and recently rediscovered her love of writing. Spending time in nature is her way to refuel and feel energized.

You can find her at:

www.beingyouenergetically.com

www.carolduttonusa.com

www.facebook.com/BeingYouEnergetically

CHAPTER 15

HOLDING SPACE DURING DEATH

PROCESSING YOUR FEELINGS WHILE EMPOWERING OTHERS TO PROCESS THEIR OWN

Robin Friend

MY STORY

"Gasp!" Startled and confused, I awakened with an unfamiliar pain radiating from my torso down each of my legs. My heart raced, and I could feel it furiously beating against the walls of my chest cavity. The bedroom was dark and chillingly cold, although the thermostat was set well above room temperature. I felt the cold settling into my entire body as if I'd been freezing for hours. I wanted to shiver, but the pain was too intense for me to react to anything else. My thoughts raced. *What is happening? Am I under attack? Is this some new form of warfare? Help! Wait, help with what? What is this?* No response. I realized I was beginning to panic. So I did what any sleep-deprived person would do under extreme levels of stress, I looked for a "Bandaid." I chose to nurture the ailment that bothers me the most— being cold—so I might find comfort in warmth and fall back to sleep.

Sleep has always been my first medicine for pain. I usually awaken feeling much better or realizing I need another dose. *This pain could use a dose of sleep, especially since it screamed loud enough to awaken me, or was it the pain that awakened me?* Well, there goes another group of thoughts to add to the dozens already racing through my mind: *Was this triggered by a dream?* The recall of my dream was foggy, but no detail. *Is everything okay?* And, then I felt a very clear response, "No, everything is not okay."

I sat up in bed, eyes opened as wide as I could, peering around the room, looking for any unusual detail, *nothing.* I continued scoping the room for cues, clues, threats, and hope; *nothing.* The pain began to slither from my muscles and ligaments, taking shelter in my bones. Unsure of how much more time remained before I needed to arise for the full day ahead, I decided to take action. *I need to get warm.* That'll help. I slid out of bed and began to stand. *Whose legs are these?* My legs were unstable and heavy. I ran my hand down my thigh in disbelief. *Feels like mine when I touch it, but not when I use it. Let's try this again.* I took a step forward and was quickly reminded that my observation was indeed accurate: *these are my legs, but they're not working like they belong to me right now.* I instinctively reached for the wall to support my balance. Scaling the wall, I led myself down the hall and opened the closet door to grab a heavy blanket. I stumbled back to the bedroom, finding warmth under the extra blanket, and drifted deep into sleep. My medicine worked.

Hours later, I awakened to only an impression of the pain I'd experienced before. To my surprise, I was greeted by something new. Doom. I'd never felt such a feeling before. I wanted to escape it. But there was no escape. I wanted to fix it. But there was no fixing what was, for there was only the presence of doom. I felt hopeless. I felt heavy. I looked at myself in the mirror and only saw a shell of me. After applying every skill I knew to comfort myself back to wholeness, only days later did I realize that it was never *my* pain I felt. It was my father's. I was meant to feel it, be with it, and hold space for him as he was experiencing it, to acknowledge his journey and support his choice to let go.

Three days later, my father passed due to complications from COVID-19. Two days following my experience, I was informed he'd been taken by ambulance to the hospital. His multiple sclerosis weakened his legs, leaving him unable to pull himself up off the cold floor. It was his second unexpected fall in the middle of the night within a week. To my surprise, the first occurred on the night of my experience. COVID pneumonia weakened his lungs, and doctors began to treat the blood clots. For me, the doom felt distant now. Yet only as distant as the hospital I could see from the street but couldn't enter. Traditional visitation was prohibited due to COVID precautions, so I opted to astral project. I was eager to speak with my father, be with him, and share space with him.

Upon arrival, I was greeted by a large group of souls surrounding the foot of my father's hospital bed. None of them wanted to make way for me to reach him, so I pushed my way through with authority. I saw him resting. His physical body was breathing, and his mind was busy processing. I began to shield him with a sphere of light so that he could rest peacefully. I sensed he had a decision to make. His body took a deep breath and released a restful sigh. My work was done. Turning to exit, I heard one of the souls waiting at his bedside shout a demand, "Heal him!" Still very clear of my authority, I responded inwardly and projected: *That is not my role; I am here to bring him peace.* I then began to review the signature of each of the energies present. There were family members, friends, and those I did not recognize, but they were present for him. And they stood with him in the non-physical as we would in the physical. I appreciated that. I exited with a comforting sense of peace.

The next day it was clear to me I needed to speak with him. I received word that he held a video call with another family member. Elated and anxious, I waited for the green light to hold my own video call. He answered, smiling, eyes bright. His light was brilliantly masking the sound of the high flow oxygen rushing through his airways. For a moment, I wasn't quite sure why I needed to speak with him. He was in great spirits. He looked well. He sounded pleasant. His energy was peaceful. Then it hit me: I'd become distracted while looking for my own reassurance and not paying attention to what he needed. This wasn't about me, although this conversation was about us. Our relationship as father and daughter dangled before our eyes. I was being asked to hold space and be present in this moment, to meet my father where he was, for him to be who he chose to be in that moment. I was there to help him feel all of what he needed to feel in the safety of neutrality. There was no right or wrong, only space. "If we can just get through this year, everything is going to be alright," he said. My mouth turned upward to form a soft smile. Then, staring into the phone, deep into his eyes, I replied, "You know you're here to live for you, not anyone else, right?" He paused briefly, clearly indicating he'd heard the question. But he dodged it with his infamous charm stating we'd talk soon. I didn't know it in that moment, but he'd make his decision later that night.

I spoke to him from a space of peace that I was unaware of consciously. I sat the phone down, feeling light and hopeful. *What was that feeling of doom all about? Meh. It doesn't really matter; it's gone now.* My phone rang hours later. My bright-eyed father had coded several times. He wasn't coming back to this life. He chose to join those who surrounded the foot of his hospital bed. He chose to walk away from doom. His body was slowly failing him, stricken by multiple sclerosis. He was riddled with pain and did an excellent job masking it. A lively man felt imprisoned in his vessel of a body. And the thought of his family potentially having to take care of his every need was not the life he wanted. Cold. Pain. Panic. Doom. The words he did not express outwardly met me in the energetic connection we shared. I honored his choice to honor himself.

It took me a while to reach that conclusion. I sat in a frozen state of grief, processing the series of events that led to this abrupt change in our world. *Did I cause this? Should I have said something different? I feel lost. Where is the "Bandaid" for this? Perhaps sleep will help.* Sleep offered me rest. Upon awakening, I felt the same, lost. I was so caught in the monologue occurring in my mind that I could only muster the strength to be the minimum of what I needed to be for my loved ones. And absolutely nothing of what I needed to be for myself. I stopped holding space the moment I got the call. I was no longer present to the world. I was merely a shadow of my true existence.

Everywhere I turned, I received a reminder to live, not only to survive but to live. There was the enthusiastic clerk at the store who happened to have my father's name. *What an infectious laugh she has.* There was the song that magically played outside of its genre reminding me of the cycles of water emphasizing new beginnings. *He loved every moment he spent on the sea.* It was time to hold space for transformation to occur with ease. It was time to hold space for myself. The world I once knew changed. Yes. And it was continuing to transform even as I resisted, making the experience more uncomfortable for me. It was time to choose: let change occur naturally or resist change with all my might. I realized that the frozen state of grief I felt was fueled by my resistance to letting go. *Sigh.* I ripped off the Bandaid.

THE TOOL

The ReSet Program is a tangible tool to guide anyone experiencing change. We all get knocked off of our axis, and there are tools to help us get back up again. From my personal experience, I've developed a program to support your reset at your own pace. All-natural intention candles serve as energy tools while the participant shifts through each phase of the program's self-guided healing experience. Relax. Relate. Release. Receive. No matter how you measure its weight on your life, the ReSet Program will hold space for you as you adjust to the comfort level you choose.

Here's a sample of how it worked for me. To begin to hold space for myself, I needed to come to center. It was time for a reset. I needed to trust in my ability to feel present with my emotions. Ignoring my emotions was the exact opposite of holding space. It was time I met myself where I was. It was time I allowed myself to just be who I was in the moment. *My father died.* I needed to say it. *My father died.* I needed to feel it. *My father died.* I needed to process it. *My father died.* I needed to accept there were more blessings waiting to be received.

The ReSet Program is designed to help you get to know yourself and how you feel as you navigate your way through life. Step by step, phase by phase, candle by candle, we ReSet our experience. The most basic level of self-care begins with self-awareness. *How do I feel?* It is of the utmost importance that we answer ourselves honestly.

I stood before the mirror, studying the figure gazing back at me, looking for my emotions and what I recognized. But a great chunk of what I identified with was no longer the same. *I feel so much right now; I don't know where to begin.* So like a child sifting through her newfound vulnerability, I flopped to the floor with my legs crossed, and I became still—pouting, yet still. Crying, and still. Surrendering. I remained still. I was still, although my mind was not yet silent. The questions began to roll like thunder. *How long will this feeling last? Am I handling this properly?* Simple responses met me at the end of my thoughts. *It will last as long as it takes me to move through it. We all handle grief in our own way. Don't rush the process—trust the process.*

Using the ReSet Program, I began to work through each emotion. Initially, I allowed myself to manage what my sensitive state of being could handle with ease and very little effort; breathing, eating, sleeping. As I became more present to my daily activities, I noticed other emotions surfacing. A flood of emotions tipped me from left to right, up and down, this way and that way. Finding stillness guided me to relax while journeying through rough waters instead of resisting the rise and fall of the sea. Eventually, in my stillness, I began to seek out every emotion—seen and unseen. No rock was left unturned. I identified how I felt in every part of my body, compartment of my mind, and aspect of my life. One by one, I called the emotions forth, and I began to work with them.

How do I feel when you are present? How do you fit into my life? This was trusting the process. The conditioning of life started unraveling before my eyes as the interviewing continued. This was turning out to be an excellent tool to navigate through uncharted waters. Death didn't knock me off of my axis, my natural resistance to change did. Grief is a natural response to loss. How we hold space for ourselves and others as we move through it is a skill.

Centering ourselves around NOW is the freedom we find in living.

Here is a ReSet Program practice to help us connect with our NOW moment. This exercise can be used anywhere and takes less than a minute to effectively bring our awareness into the present moment for centering. It can be used as often as needed.

BE HERE NOW brief exercise to RELAX

Hold your hand out approximately six inches from your face with your palm facing you. Use your eyes to trace the outside of your hand as if your eyes are the chalk outlining your hand in the air, up and down, and around the curves of your fingers. Now study the lines in your palms and locate your fingerprints. Those are yours! This is your hand. Flip your hand over and review the backside of your hand. Move your fingers any way you choose. These are your fingers. They are responding to you. You are present in this moment. Welcome back to your body. Welcome back to the center of now. Welcome back to how it feels to be you in this human experience.

After taking inventory of how I felt with my own emotions, it became easy to see how others felt. Separating the emotion from the individual, the feeling from the situation, and the situation from the response, removed any form of judgment for someone else's way of processing death. I saw the pain in their actions. I heard the sadness in their words. I chose to remain still. I chose to be present with them without trying to "fix" them. For they were never broken, they were processing in their own way. I was now actively holding space for others even as I continued to move through my own grief. I met them where they were and allowed them to be who they were as they felt what they felt. Every emotion arrives to offer us an experience. We consciously choose how we feel it.

Releasing something before you know how it serves you may present its own form of resistance. That anger may just fuel your strength once you get to know how it fits into your life. That sadness may spark your gratitude as you review the memories you share with your deceased loved one. I learned not to be so quick to get beyond the liminal space of transformation by trusting the process I gained from it.

Robin Friend is the founder and owner of Eleven Eleven Candles and More, LLC and Sacred Soul Work, LLC. She started her journey as a spiritual practitioner in 2018 when she began creating intention candles. Soon after, she became a Master Intention Candle Artist while freely exploring her abilities. She has since become a reiki practitioner and has worked with spiritual leaders to further develop her gifts. She now serves as a healing artist, medium, and soul work priestess offering an array of products and services, including interactive workshops, intention products, intuitive consultations, and sacred ceremonies. Robin is often referred to as a "way-shower," a term used by indigenous cultures for those who lead simply by living an authentic life. Her goal is to provide a safe haven for souls while sharing ancient wisdom and spiritual practices to elevate our thinking, our actions, and our view of self within modern society to a higher level of consciousness. All are welcome to explore how to reset their reality by visiting www.eleven-eleven-candles.com. There is a safe haven that is ready to support your journey.

CHAPTER 16

RADICAL SELF-CARE FOR CAREGIVERS

NOURISHING YOURSELF THROUGH GRIEF AND LOSS

Kelly Myerson, MA, OTR

MY STORY

Digging through piles of paper and receipts, it was hard to know what was meaningful and what needed to go into the recycling. Perched on top of a pile of clothes, papers, and other items, I pulled out an overstuffed drawer.

Inside among the many crossed-off to-do lists were letters. And not just any letters, letters written between my grandparents while my grandfather was stationed in France during World War II. I cradled them in my hands and introduced myself to versions of my grandparents a few years younger than I was at that moment. My parents, aunt, sister, cousin, and I found many treasures going through my grandparents' home, but to me, these were the most precious.

"What are those, Kelly?" My cousin Stephanie walked over to me wearing a gold lamé jacket. The shoulder pads made the shirt look even larger on her small frame.

My grandmother stood at six feet tall and had the most amazing fashion! She stockpiled nearly all her clothes from the 1950s to the 80s, and my sister Jill, Stephanie, and I loved diving into her racks of clothes in the basement. We'd dash up the basement steps with our arms overflowing with polyester garments. "Alright, let's have a show and tell," my grandmother would say.

Still, she required the last say on whether we could take pieces or had to return them to the racks. "Oh, no, that one you'll have to put back," she'd shake her head and point down the basement stairs.

Does she really think she'll wear them again? I thought to myself as my eyes rolled, and I reluctantly returned the pieces with which she couldn't bear to part.

Now, I held out a letter to Stephanie with tears in my eyes. "Steph, these are love letters from Grandma and Grandpa."

Stephanie reached out and took it gently in her hands. We wordlessly looked at each other with tears falling softly down our cheeks. For once, we were grateful that my grandmother kept nearly everything; treasures and trash were gathered together in great groups in every room of their home.

My grandfather passed away a few years prior, and my grandmother could no longer live on her own. Sadly, her mind had begun to succumb to Alzheimer's.

Closing my eyes, I felt the familiar tug of sadness in my chest. *Grandpa, I miss you so much.*

His voice as he used to greet me in his doorway echoed through my head.

"Hello, Kelly!" he'd cheer with enthusiasm and a joyful smile. His arms would enfold me in a tight squeeze. His hugs made me feel like the most treasured person in the world. He smiled with his eyes. Actually, I think he smiled with his whole being. His warmth radiated around him. We all felt it, all ten grandchildren and two great-grandchildren.

Stepping into their tiny entryway, I could pick up the familiar buzz of a soap opera—my grandmother's "stories"—playing in the background. Looking to the right over the half wall, I could see the dining room and living room where my entire family would gather on Christmas to open great piles of presents. Grandma would announce, "Okay, everyone, time for show and tell." We'd dutifully hold up each object to the group.

Turning back to the kitchen, I'd watch Grandma methodically bustling around, returning every few minutes to her to-do list, jotted on the back of a receipt, to cross off an item.

Grandpa would pour me a cup of coffee and gesture to me to sit at the kitchen table. When he presented me with a fresh coffee cake, he'd know what was coming next.

"John!" my grandmother would scold, exasperated. "There's a coffee cake from yesterday!"

"No, Francine," he'd state, shaking his head, "I'm giving her the fresh one." I wonder if he delighted in defying Grandma's frugal nature. Delicious decisions; my grandpa was good at those.

Life with Grandpa was always sweet, literally. He had a sweet tooth which his ten grandchildren all inherited. No visit was complete without Grandpa opening a new Almond Ring or a fresh box of chocolates. Then, bowing his head for a minute, he would pray over every meal and snack wordlessly. He never commanded anyone to join him; it was his silent devotion and commitment to gratitude for every morsel he ate.

Sitting at the kitchen table overlooking his backyard, I would look out at his beautiful garden while my mouth filled with the sweetness of almond paste and frosting.

Looking up from his coffee, Grandpa noticed me looking outside. "Today, we're going to repaint the picnic table and benches," he instructed with a smile.

To date, Grandpa is still my best employer. He would pay me for a day's labor toiling in his garden and painting the patio furniture to keep it looking crisp. Beginning the day with coffee and cake was typical. I'd also look forward to the well-placed breaks: lunch at noon, tea and snacks at 3 pm, followed by cocktails at 5, and dinner at 6 pm.

Brownie, my grandfather's dog, looked up as we stood to go outside. Brownie looked more like a Twinkie, for he would have a heaping bowl of ice cream after dinner every night because, according to my grandpa, "he liked it."

On the steps to the garage, the smells of gasoline and motor oil mixed with Grandpa's fresh sunscreen met my nose. Grandpa handed me a can of paint and a couple of paintbrushes. Stepping outside, he unlatched the gate to his backyard. Where there was once an in-ground pool now resided the most beautiful garden that ended at a gazebo. Grandpa was a true Dutchman, and his garden was his work of living art. Hues of every color of the rainbow met my eyes. Plants were spaced so you could walk among them.

"We're going to freshen up this table and benches," he instructed. "Take care not to use too much paint, so it won't bubble. Like this." He dipped a brush into the paint, precisely removing any excess and carefully moving the brush up and down.

I took a brush and repeated his steps. He smiled. "You got it!"

He left me to paint while he lovingly got his hands in the dirt and tended to his plants. The smell of earth reached my nose as I watched Grandpa silently assessing what each bed needed: water, weeding, or feeding. I tried my best to match his care and precision as I painted.

A little while later, he broke our silent work to announce, "Okay, time for lunch. I picked up some fresh buns and ham for lunch. Let's see if any of the tomatoes are ready to be picked." He would always select the ripest Jersey tomato from the plants and bring it in to wash.

Slicing into the tomato, he offered me a piece for my sandwich. Grandma handed me a glass of iced tea half-filled with ice. Cold liquid washed down my throat, cooling me from our time in the sun.

Our break over, we returned to our work until it was time for tea and more treats. After tea, Grandpa quietly retreated to his bedroom for his daily nap while I headed back outside to peacefully finish painting. At the end of the day, he thanked me and handed me a hundred-dollar bill. Every time, I'd see the delight in his eyes for having had time with me, and I was equally filled with gratitude.

Even as I write this, I tear up because all the time I had with him will never be enough.

In the summer of 2004, as my family was getting ready for my sister Jill's wedding, my grandpa drove himself to the hospital. His stomach had been feeling off; we're not sure how long he had been feeling sick.

"There's a tumor the size of a grapefruit in his belly," I remember my mom gently telling me. The doctors had explained it was growing rapidly.

Just as we gathered for Christmas at my grandparents' home, my family all gathered in the hospital, enough of us to crowd the hallway. Somber, we were each given time to go in and hold his hand and say our goodbyes.

I walked into the ICU room as the monitors beeped each beat of his heart. Taking his hand in mine, my eyes traced his still face. The palms of his hands felt rough, weathered from the work he loved. Though he wasn't awake, I knew he could feel and hear me there.

"Grandpa, I love you. It's okay to go," I wept. But inside, I was screaming,

Please get better; please stay, don't leave yet!

He did stay, just a few weeks longer. He passed a day after my sister's wedding, his last gift of generosity. He truly put others first.

I wasn't there when my grandpa passed or when my family laid him to rest; circumstances and attempts to fix a broken marriage had me miles away. In my absence, I sent my eulogy in his honor. I filled it with stories and memories to comfort my family. My grandpa was one of my heroes. He lit up the world by being in it. He sought simple joy—time in nature, with his dogs, connected to his family, and praising God for all His blessings. He savored life, and I learned to do the same from him.

What we came to discover after he passed was my grandmother's mounting forgetfulness. Her idiosyncrasies began to appear more malignant. My dad noticed her asking the same questions over and over, and she'd perseverate on one topic.

We realized my grandfather had likely managed her memory lapses by keeping their daily and weekly routines consistent. He had been caretaking not only for his home and garden but also for his beloved wife. Though he wasn't writing her letters, his actions spoke to his great love and devotion to my grandmother.

Caring for a loved one who is gradually losing their battle with a disease may be an experience that resonates with you. Maybe you have felt overwhelmed. Maybe you're feeling a loss of self.

I shared my grandpa's story because I see the many subtle lessons in wellness and self-care in the way he lived his life. I'm not sure he intended to be a teacher, but I was his willing pupil. Let me share some of his wisdom with you.

If you'd like to see some pictures of him, visit https://beingwellwithkelly.com/sacreddeathresources/.

THE TOOL

In the beginning of 2019, I set the intention to prioritize my self-care. After years of downplaying my own needs and frequently succumbing to the effects of ignoring my body, I was ready to exist in a state of wellness.

Then in March 2020, I faltered. Like many working moms, I took on the role of working from home while facilitating my son's education under the stress of the unknown. Committed to doing everything perfectly, I lasted about two weeks before mental and physical exhaustion caught up with me.

Overwhelmed, I called my husband at work sobbing. He helped to calm me, and later on, we sat down and decided, as a family, that we needed to prioritize our mental health and physical wellbeing. We shifted from following all the expectations of work and school to putting our sleep, rest, and nutrition first. We hadn't ever set family expectations on our health, but it was transformative.

I decided to develop a framework of a few things I could do every day to maintain my sanity and my wellbeing. As you care for a loved one who is in their final stages in life or deal with loss and grief, may this tool be one way for you to care for yourself.

The framework includes: Ten minutes of movement, five minutes of stillness, three items on a to-do list, and one connection to someone who supports you every day. You can find a visual of this framework and an expansion on my resource page at https://beingwellwithkelly.com/sacreddeathresources/.

10 MINUTES OF MOVEMENT

You may be thinking, *is ten minutes enough?* In most circumstances, probably not. However, when you feel overwhelmed, you need to find ways to take care of yourself that are manageable or even easy.

Take ten minutes to move your body in any way you love. Do yoga or gentle stretching, go for a walk, dance to your favorite music, or even tend to your own garden—just move in a way that is fun for you.

5 MINUTES OF STILLNESS

Be still and breathe. Keep it simple. You can certainly listen to a guided meditation or even go for longer. But what if all you had to do was commit to five minutes to yourself to breathe and be still at the beginning of your day? Feels possible, right?

In stillness, place your hand on your heart. Ask yourself, *dear one, what do you need?* Then, bravely and boldly offer yourself what it is you need. Is it rest, connection, some water, a good meal, a hot shower, or something else?

Check out some of my recommendations for music
and guided meditation on my resource page
https://beingwellwithkelly.com/sacreddeathresources/.

3 ITEMS ON YOUR TO-DO LIST

I know what you're thinking; you have way more than three things to do every day. You probably have dozens. Brain-dump your whole list and boil it down to your top three priorities. Now, write them as results—what will this task look like when it's complete? Then, check back on your list for what can be delegated and *ask* for help.

1 CONNECTION WITH SOMEONE WHO SUPPORTS YOU

As a caregiver, you're used to being the support, not needing it. Your fourth priority is to reach out every day to one person who is available to support you. Maybe this person can take on some of the items you chose to delegate. Maybe they can be a sounding board for your sorrow or frustrations. Reach out. Share how you feel and ask for what you need.

Grief and loss are seasons for many of us. Some of us live in the season for so much longer. Take ten minutes of movement, five minutes of stillness, three to-do list items, and one connection to a support person daily to carry you through. When you are sinking in the overwhelm, reach out.

I have a special message for you. Please visit my resource page to hear it. https://beingwellwithkelly.com/sacreddeathresources/.

Kelly is an author, speaker, coach, and sleep expert who will cultivate space for you to emerge from stress and overwhelm to lead and savor the life of your dreams. As an occupational therapist, Kelly has over 20 years of experience specializing in sensory integration techniques. Her background in occupational therapy provides a unique perspective on development and the human condition. She helps overwhelmed working moms light up the world by taking them from burned out to radiating joy.

With a Master's degree in Strategic Communication and Leadership, she brings data-driven techniques leading to lasting change. Over the past 15 years, she has experience teaching topics including self-care, leadership development, outcome measurement, sensory processing related to anxiety, and sleep. Kelly is a holistic entrepreneur bringing a wealth of experience and fun science to inspire her clients. Most importantly, she'll get you the best night of sleep ever! You can check out her recent chapters, *Sacred Sleep: Cultivating the Best Sleep of Your Life* in the best-selling book, <u>The Ultimate Guide to Self-Healing, Volume 4</u> and *Courageous Self-care: Putting Myself First to Serve Others* in <u>Find Your Voice Save Your Life Volume 2</u>. Both available at https://beingwellwithkelly.com/books/.

For resources related to Kelly's healing journey and to connect with her, please visit https://www.beingwellwithkelly.com

CHAPTER 17
EMBODIED AWARENESS

USING CONTEMPLATION, ACUPRESSURE, AND BREATH TO RELEASE CHARGED EMOTIONS

Dr. Alice Feng, MBBS

MY STORY

My grandmother (Pópo 婆婆) was my rock, my everything. When I received the news from home that my grandmother was diagnosed with lung cancer, my heart was in shock and disbelief. My heart ached, and I longed to be physically close to her.

She never acted like she had cancer and was still living her life as if she was cancer-free and even flew to Shanghai, China to visit me and see the World Expo. We had a scare one day when her lungs started to fill up with fluid and took her to the emergency room. I felt overwhelmed and helpless seeing all the trauma patients being rolled into the ER all night, one after another, hearing the excruciating moans of pain.

I realized working at a corporate job didn't feel right to me; I wanted to be of service, support, and care for people. Spending the night in the ER was my opportunity to take care of Pópo. I'm grateful to have had one of the most life-changing conversations with Pópo that night; I told her my idea to apply for medical school to become a Chinese Medicine physician, and she fully supported me.

Several months after my Pópo flew back to Chicago, I matriculated at Shanghai University of Traditional Chinese Medicine with a full government scholarship. Along with my school studies, I also studied with highly skilled acupuncturists and herbalists on the weekends outside of school to gain more clinical experience. I was so busy with my medical studies I buried the reality of Pópo dying with all the uncomfortable emotions that came with it into my subconscious for several years. If I didn't think about it, then I was 'alright.' I held this bracing pattern in my emotional body until the pressure building inside burst all this emotive lava up and out like a volcano! The trigger was when I got a call from home to fly back ASAP because Pópo's health was deteriorating quickly. After I hung up the phone, I suddenly felt an intense burning ache in my heart; an array of emotions bubbled up to the surface, piercing my being like a million daggers. I was overwhelmed. I had no idea where all these emotions came from and didn't have the resources to support me to move through them. I was a pro at stuffing down my emotions, it was my default coping mechanism.

Feeling extremely raw and vulnerable, I flew back home to be with Pópo. I felt guilty that I couldn't do much to relieve her pain and suffering. The painkillers were doing their job, but they also dulled her mind, and I wasn't able to connect with her in the way I wanted to; that sucked! This left me feeling frustrated and deeply sad. The feeling of regret washed over me as I ruminated on time lost not being with her when she had a sound mind. She could not talk and rarely opened her eyes.

One evening, all the grandchildren gathered around her and sang *Take Me Home, Country Roads*, and we saw a teardrop roll down her cheek; she could still hear and sense our presence and love for her. At that moment, that was all the validation I needed. She heard and felt her beloved family beside her, in the comfort of her home. The night she transitioned from the earth plane back Home to source, I had a strong intuitive feeling it would happen and slept at the edge of her bed. When I felt no pulse, I made the difficult phone call to tell the rest of the family she was in the process of transitioning. Today, the grief of missing her physical presence and wanting to feel the warmth of her snuggles and laugh with her is still there. The intense emotional charge of sadness, grief, and guilt subsided when I took frequent pauses to contemplate, check in with myself, dropped into my body and used breath guided acupressure to support the process of emotional release.

THE TOOL

The practice of contemplation, self-inquiry, acupressure massage with intentional breathing and "the drop supported me in reframing the narrative of being a helpless victim controlled by my emotions, especially the grief of losing my beloved grandmother. Identifying the false narratives I carried created space for me to anchor into my sovereignty to empower me to be the master of my charged emotions. As a recovering emotion stuffer, I allowed for intentional moments of pause to just be with whatever charged emotions arose and felt the nuanced expressions from the soft to the hard edges. Over time, taking frequent mindful pauses in my day became spontaneous gaps for contemplation; when I'm strolling on the beach, walking through a forest preserve trail, sitting on the grass, journaling, dancing, cooking, or meditating. I delighted in these pauses that lead to inner transformation over time.

THE ART OF CONTEMPLATION:

"Every pause is a field of transformation."

~Richard Rudd

Pause: Bring awareness to the present moment and simply be with the presence of the emotion(s) that arises.

Allow: Allow yourself to feel the charge of the pain in the emotion you're experiencing. Simply allow yourself to feel it. You don't have to like or even become best buddies with them.

Accept: Acknowledge that emotions are apart of your human experience. Provide some breathing space and accept it is here to be felt, expressed, and not intellectualized or overanalyzed until the cows come home! Allow space to fully feel into the discomfort of the emotion(s), getting comfortable with the discomfort of the emotional charge that may feel overwhelming and scary and making you feel frustrated or irritated. The tendency of our mind to create elaborate narratives from past experiences create the charge attached to emotions. Be patient with yourself; you're doing deep inner work transforming old wound patterns and shifting the way you relate to charged emotions and yourself. Repairing and rebuilding a new relationship with your emotions require patience and trust; it is a process.

Embodied Acceptance Practice: Gently place the palms of your hands over your lower belly (Dantian 'energy center') just below the navel; bring your awareness here. Inhale through your nose and visualize expansive space permeating your mind-body-spirit. Exhale, softening the intensity of the charge in the emotion. With each cycle of breath, soften a little bit deeper until you feel a sense of ease in your being. Just be here, for the moment. Rest in this space you have created for yourself.

Reframe and Pivot: Identify the stories and limiting false beliefs that are not serving your overall well-being. An opportunity to pivot arises within the pause. Pivoting can quickly change the mood we're in from a downward slide to an upward spiral, increasing our frequency with the quality of our thoughts. Awareness shines light on the possibility of making a different decision in any given moment, thus changing our thoughts that affect our biology and physiology.

Embrace: Integrate the charged emotions as a part of you with you in the driver's seat and the emotions in the backseat, taking a moment to pause and breathe into this 'now' moment. Feel your feet touching the ground and orient yourself inwards. Deeply trust (consciously and subconsciously) the decisions you make and know they're not etched in stone; you can pivot and make a new decision anytime. Qi ('omnipresent life force') flows to where your attention is placed; your thoughts create your reality.

*"When emotions are expressed, all systems are united and made whole.
When emotions are repressed, denied, not allowed to be whatever
they may be, our network pathways get blocked,
stopping the flow of the vital feel-good, unifying chemicals
that run both our biology and our behavior."*

~Candice B. Pert

CONTEMPLATIVE SELF-INQUIRY:

Hold these questions lightly, allowing an answer to unfold in its own time without forcing it.

What narratives do I carry in this emotion I am experiencing?

How do these stories feel in my body?

What is the quality of the charge in the emotions I am experiencing?

If your tears could talk, what would they say to you?

What is my sigh indicating to me right now?

What am I up to right now?

Am I willing to make a different decision?

Am I in command, or are my emotions running the show?

Do I believe I am a victim of my emotional waves?

Where can I be more gentle with myself?

Where can I create more space for grace?

Will I honor and regard where I am at in this here and now moment?

The charge carried within emotions may hold stories of old patterns of fear, doubt, anger, pride, jealousy, or, fill in the blank_____. When we attach and grasp tightly to the past, we place shackles of limitation upon ourselves that keep us from moving forward creating stagnation in our mind and body. It is a courageous act to let go of the past, to reframe, pivot, and redirect your attention from an external orientation to an inward gaze anchored in your sovereignty, congruence and compassionate regard for yourself; when you do this, you reclaim your power back and create different neural pathways in your brain that will positively impact the reality of your existence. You're a sovereign being with free will to decide at any given moment what you intend and want for yourself to experience. Is it more ease, joy, peace and love? Are you willing to engage in your own responsibility to make different decisions that activate a paradigm shift; changing the color palette of false belief narratives attached to old patterns that paint your current worldview?

EMBODIED PRACTICE: THE DROP

When you feel overwhelmed by emotion(s) or feel a 50-foot emotional wave rising, take a moment and pause and bring your attention back into your physical body. Take a seated position with the soles of your feet anchored to the earth. Raise your hands above your shoulders and start shaking until your head and body begins to rock back and forth. When you feel you have shaken off the emotional charge, take a deep breath through your nose and drop your hands on your lap with a big exhale through your mouth. Suspend any judgments you may have and simply just be in your body, rest, and relax into this moment. When you feel grounded, ask yourself the question, *"what am I up to right now?"*

There will be moments where you feel overwhelmed and moments where you will have the capacity to be with emotions and not allow them to consume you; you're human. Be gentle with yourself and have compassion and grace for this process of grieving.

ACUPRESSURE MASSAGE WITH INTENTIONAL BREATHING:

When emotional waves come and go, on the surface, you may feel sad, anxious, angry, frightened, or shocked. You're in some kind of mood and you can sense it. In Chinese Medicine, mood is considered to be at the Wei (surface) level. When you receive the news of a loved one that passed away, that can cause you to collapse into shock, anger, sadness, or grief in varying combinations.

From the lens of Chinese Medicine, sudden, intense, prolonged emotional stimuli will cause dysfunction in the proper circulation of Qi, blood, and the organ system. A disharmony (excess or deficient state) of these seven emotions can directly affect the corresponding organs to bring on diseases causing internal injuries:

Joy (over-excitement, manic) excessive joy impairs the heart.

Anger (rage, resentment, frustration) impairs the liver.

Worry or pensiveness impairs the spleen.

Grief or sadness impairs the lung.

Fear and fright impair the kidneys.

Emotions (energy in motion) have a directionality associated with them from a Chinese Medicine energetic/Qi dynamic perspective. Anger causes the Qi to ascend, joy makes the Qi sluggish, grief depletes the Qi, fear descends the Qi, and fright scatters the Qi. Researchers have found the dysfunction in ascending and descending of Qi will change breathing rhythms in response to fluctuations in emotion such as fear, anxiety, sadness, and happiness.

Intentional acupressure may support you in moving through and releasing charged emotions and bring you back to a certain level of homeostasis. With awareness, place your attention on the acupuncture point and breathe into the area of the point corresponding with the particular emotion while using a gentle sustained pressure massaging for 3-5 minutes with your thumb or middle finger with the index finger on top to reduce strain and injury.

Grief: LI6 "Diverging Passageway" (Location: Three inches above the crease of the wrist in the direction of the shoulder)

Fear: BL58 "Taking Flight" (Location: Seven inches directly above UB 60 on the posterior border of the fibula)

Anger: GB37 "Bright Light" (Location: Five inches above the tip of the external malleolus on the anterior border of the fibula)

Obsession/Worry: ST40 "Bountiful Bulge" (Location: Eight inches above the outer ankle bone, in the depression on the outer aspect of the lower leg)

Anxiety: SI7 "Upright Branch" (Location: Five inches proximal to the dorsal crease of the wrist)

May you be gentle and patient and regard yourself with COMPASSION and grace on this healing journey. Remember, it's a process, not a destination to arrive at, nor is there anything to fix. Intentionally create time and space for REST so that you may be with your charged emotions and simply allow its expression to unfold as you move through it. I use these tools to support and facilitate emotional releases for my clients. If you need support feel free to reach out and connect with me at https://justbreathewithme.com/.

The contemplation practices are adapted from Richard Rudd's book, *The Art of Contemplation: Gentle path to wholeness and prosperity.* This is a great resource if you want to deepen your understanding of contemplation as a skillful art that expands your awareness and brings you closer in touch with your heart. Parts of the Acupressure points with intentional breathing section is based on a Daoist Chinese medical perspective transmitted by Dr. Jeffrey C. Yuen. To help you locate the acupuncture points you can go to this website https://theory.yinyanghouse.com/ and select the Acu Points tab to search for the specific acupoints (acupuncture points).

Alice Feng is trained as a Chinese Medicine Physician. She studied in five-year Chinese medical degree program at Shanghai University of Traditional Chinese Medicine and obtained her MBBS degree (equivalent to an MD degree in the US). To deepen her knowledge and clinical experience, she traveled extensively in Asia to learn from many accomplished Chinese Medicine physicians skilled in: Acupuncture, Acupressure, Herbs, Guasha, Moxibustion, diet therapy/nutrition, Qigong, Taichi, and meditation. She is also an Usui Reiki practitioner, JFB Myofascial Release therapist, and Yang Sheng nourishing life coach. She is skilled at empathetic listening, empathy, congruence, and unconditional positive regard. As a coach, Alice empowers her clients to anchor into their sovereignty, befriend their will, bring embodied awareness to charged emotions that need release so they can come back home to their true Self (original nature). She guides, supports, and regards what her clients have as they reframe their old shadow patterns—often charged with emotions and colored by false belief narratives—into gifts and possibility, and to make different decisions that support their body, mind, spirit, and soul. She holds a safe space for each person's unfolding as they heal and transform shadows into gifts as they orient inwards, journeying back into the essence of who they truly are. She meets each client where they are at, in the moment, with what they have.

Learn more about her and how to work with her at www.justbreathewithme.com.

CHAPTER 18

LETTING GO

A POWERFUL PATH TO SELF-COMPASSION AND RESPONSIBILITY

Theodora Elena Engelhart, BSc (WU)

MY STORY

22.05.2021, Guatemala

We humans are cyclic beings, and therefore we experience all four seasons every month. Winter is when a woman is bleeding; it's the season associated with stillness, transformation, death. It's a time for letting go and setting intentions for the next cycle. After winter, we welcome spring, the season of awakening, blooming, rebirth. It might be just a coincidence, or maybe it was meant to coincide with nature's changing course. But the life chapter I'm about to share with you is about death, and it started in winter 2011.

That night in winter 2011, I forgot to put my phone on mute, so it started ringing in the cinema hall, and I wouldn't have realized it was mine if my boyfriend hadn't made me aware of it. I was so excited to finally see *Black Swan*. I wanted to reject the phone call, but I saw it was from my sister and felt I should pick up. In a very quiet voice, I tried to explain to her that I was in the cinema and would call her back later. She would not let me finish my sentence, replying: "Come home! Mama tried to kill herself."

I know how much words can affect and touch us, especially when they carry deep emotions or relate to people we love. You probably had a strange feeling while reading the words of my sister; maybe it made you shudder. Those words were already part of my habitat, part of my body and mind. Because it was not the first time I'd heard them. I can't count how often I heard those words out of my mother's mouth that year. But it was still strange to hear them from my sister, so short and precise, but representing a person's current reality, a connection between a mother and daughter, a wife and husband, a human being and wounded inner child.

"Again? She has already tried so many times. I'm at the cinema right now. I will come afterward."

"No, Theo, you should come now. This time it's serious. The doctors are here.

Please come."

I will never forget that moment in the cinema, only getting to see the advertisements and annoyed faces of the people sitting next to me and my boyfriend's face already knowing what I would tell him. He grabbed my hand and took me to the car. I can't remember how we got home or opened the door and entered the house. I just remember hearing my grandfather screaming from his bed: "Please stop her." My grandfather, my mother's father, wished he could stop her had he still been able to walk and stand by himself. I don't know how long he was screaming, but his voice sounded depleted. Some moments are so blurred, and others so crystal clear.

The moment it hit me the most, I was standing in front of my room, the door wide open, my mother lying on the floor with her feet facing the door, and her body very close to my desk. Around her was the ambulance staff and doctor, who I'd seen before when my mother had a trial. That time he couldn't do much for her because she was still conscious and refused his help. He looked at me. I looked at him. He said, "don't worry, she is stable now." I then looked at my mom; her eyes were open. She looked at me with that expression of a small child after being foolish and knowing they have done something "bad" but needing forgiveness and compassion. She was so close to fulfilling her wish, but at the same time, I could see fear in her eyes, realizing what could have happened if my father hadn't turned around and come straight home to find her. She planned it so well. Nobody was at home except for my grandfather, who, being captive in his bed, could not do much against her wish and could not stop her.

For some time, I stood there looking at her, how she was lying in her own urine, surrounded by all those people wearing the red suits I got to see so often that year.

My mother injected herself with insulin without having diabetes, so her blood sugar level sank dramatically. Serious hypoglycemia (<40 mg/dl) can have severe consequences, including ending in a coma and dying. When the ambulance came, my mother had only 20 mg/dl in her blood. When I arrived, they had already injected glucose to increase and stabilize her blood sugar level.

While I kept looking at my mother, I felt trapped in my own body. I couldn't even lean towards her or hold her. I stood there looking at her lying in my room. *Why was she in my room?* At the same moment, I heard the doctor telling me to look at my laptop, "Your mother left you a letter." I went straight to my desk and saw the screen still on. There were a lot of words on that screen. I sat down and started reading. *It must have taken her some time to write all those pages.*

I was the only one she thought of writing to. She asked me for forgiveness and tried to help me understand that I should take care of myself the way she should have but couldn't anymore. I was 17 years old and living in a new country for three years, a country where love brought us and gave us an amazing family. She had a loving husband. I had a father I'd always wished for and three step-siblings. We finally found a home and endless care and love. But it was not enough.

How can peace and true love find a safe place in your life if you are fighting a war within?

I read my mother's words several times while she was being prepared to be taken to the hospital.

That night I couldn't sleep. I kept looking in the dark at the place next to my bed, where I could still feel my mother's energy and picture the whole scene in my head. I didn't cry that night. It might sound strange, but that night, even though I couldn't sleep, I felt a little bit of lightness in my chest. I felt happiness and release. I knew that no matter how hard the next months would be for all of us, my mother would be cared for and receive the help she needed.

While I'm putting my experience into words, I feel how much of this chapter of life is still stored in my body and mind. I feel like traveling with a time machine and reliving every little detail again. I would not say I'm wiser or would have acted differently or known more; it's just that I can look at it from a different perspective. But now I feel very proud of both parts of me. I'm proud of the 17-year-old Theodora for facing an intense chapter in life and accepting the wish of her mother, even if it would mean losing her in the physical world.

She learned after months of repeatedly hearing, "I am going to kill myself," and several trials trying to convince her mother of the options and solutions, that they could get through it together, the way they managed all other obstacles in their life, that it's not about her. She learned it's not about her mother not loving her, not her fault, and that she needs to let go. She learned to let go of how she wanted her mother to see the world and of blaming her for her decisions. She had to let go of her ego and take responsibility for her own life while understanding she couldn't control or change others. But she *could* decide how she responded to every situation life is offering her.

She decided to accept her mother's wish and be aware that at some point, it could become a reality. But she also decided to love her mother without judgment still. She understood that the suffering we feel when we lose someone is because of our own demands and wishes. It's because we can't see/touch/have this person here with us anymore. It's all about us wanting to control everything in our life, including the lives of others and their decisions. She understood that in her case, the best way she could help her mother was to give her compassion, forgiveness, and love unconditionally. And as painful as letting go can be, it's what allows us to grow, transform, and thrive.

Out of that transformation and process of surrendering, I'm also proud of today's 28-year-old Theodora for having the courage to step into her trauma and share it with the world as part of her healing. Without this part of me and my life, I wouldn't have been able to guide and support others in their process of letting go the way I'm doing today.

Spring 2012

After a long and intense winter, with not only school tasks but also household responsibilities and many other challenging situations, spring finally arrived. And at the same time, my mother returned home.

Her energy changed. I could see through her eyes that more calmness found its place in her heart. Although we all were more than happy to have my mother back home, the fear it might happen again was still stored within us.

One of the main reasons my mother would commit suicide was because she was not feeling worthy or needed anymore. As a single mother, she would care for her parents and me, working hard to pay all the bills and provide for us. Because of her very intense job and our family situation, she was constantly in fight-or-flight mode. This job exposed her to a lot of mental and physical trauma.

When my mother met my stepfather, she finally found a precious guardian and lover who would take away some weight off her shoulders, allowing her to slow down. She would not need to function the way she used to.

But because she was not used to slowing down or allowing herself to heal, everything came at once, too fast to be accepted or processed sustainably by her mind and body. And therefore, her depressive mood became deeper and harder to understand.

As we all wanted to prevent another relapse, we started brainstorming about how we could support my mother in feeling worthy enough and giving her the chance to develop further. My mother's dream since childhood was to create a retirement home for her grandparents. We didn't create a retirement home, but together we started a caregiver agency. I remember how much fun I had in finding a name, creating the logo, and writing the text for the booklets. This project started purely out of love, without any expectations of expanding or bringing profits.

Nevertheless, today my mother's agency is working with 50 families and providing 100 caregivers a workplace, everything being managed by my mother. She is healthy, and sometimes, because of being the biggest empath I know, she stresses herself way too much trying to make this world a better place. It's not always easy, every day brings new challenges, but I feel we are walking on the right path, and together we support each other, even if it is not always visible. The energy and space we created between us connect us no matter where we find ourselves in the physical realm.

I try to construct my life upon the idea that nothing is permanent, that everything is constantly changing. Living as a cyclic being means I must acknowledge impermanence for its beauty and embrace the power of allowing us to let go, transform, be present, and not try to control everything.

THE TOOL

Long before coming in touch with the practice of yoga and meditation, during my childhood, I developed a tool to connect to myself and work through my emotions. I call it the "mirrored me." This technique helped me to support the process of letting go and it's still playing a vital role in my life today. It can be used as a daily ritual just for a few minutes or, when needed, for longer.

I invite you to find yourself in front of a mirror, a big mirror, where you can see yourself entirely is optimal, but not necessary. You should be able to at least see your head and your upper body.

Start by finding a comfortable sitting or standing position. Relax your shoulders, relax your face and start with acknowledging how your body is grounding through your feet (standing) or through your sitting bones. Bring your awareness to your face and start looking into your eyes, as you would look into the eyes of the person you love the most. Let all your thoughts pass by and focus only on your breath and your eyes. Try to observe your eyes and, at the same time, be aware of how your upper body is moving with every inhalation and exhalation. You can deepen the breath and arrive in your body more, into the space being created and the connection with your eyes.

Whenever you feel you need a break, I invite you to close your eyes while remaining present.

Take as much time as you need for this practice and allow yourself to enter into this connection with yourself from a place of self-compassion, being proud of yourself for doing this work. I also invite you to place your hands onto your heart space in the center of your chest. Remain in this state of eye contact with yourself as long as you need. With every inhale, let your breath flow down into your belly and let your belly expand. With every exhale, let the air flow back from your belly to your chest and outside your body. Let go of all the air inside of you, making space for new, fresh air and trusting the next inhale will follow with ease.

Before taking your next inhale, think of an emotion, situation, or person you want to let go of. Something that is not serving you any longer on your journey. Start your intention with "I let go of …" I encourage you to say your intention out loud to manifest it stronger. Say your intention while looking into your own eyes. Take a deep inhale, feel the presence and power of your words and intention. With the exhale, send your intention through your eyes into the eyes of your reflection. Go through at least five cycles of breath and the letting go intention before moving to another intention or ending the practice.

Acknowledge if you feel any changes in your body while doing this exercise. Our emotions are stored in different parts of our bodies, so sometimes, you might feel a part of your body more intensely than another. If this is the case, bring your focus to that part, and with every exhale, release the tension.

When you feel like you want to end your practice, I invite you to close your eyes for a moment and come one more time into a present posture. Feel once again your connection to the earth through your feet or sitting bones and bring your hands in prayer in front of your chest. With your eyes closed or open, while looking at yourself, thank yourself for the space you've created, for your courage in facing your fears, emotions, and imperfection, and in doing the work of letting go, not only for yourself but also for those around you. Be proud of yourself, as you would be of the person you love the most. Give yourself a last, big hug and a smile and promise yourself to take good care of yourself. Come back to this practice as often as you need to and let it guide you towards the best version of yourself.

Looking into someone's eyes, including our own, can be very overwhelming and awaken many different emotions. During my current study in psychotherapy, I learned that when we experience eye contact, our brain and endocrine system are starting to produce the happiness hormone called Oxytocin. Oxytocin is known for its power to regulate emotions, including lowering stress and anxiety and supporting the parasympathetic nervous system in relaxing and regenerating itself. It's no coincidence that this technique has served me so deeply all these years.

Theodora was born on a summer day in 1992 in Romania. She moved at 15 years to Austria, where she studied Economics and Socioeconomics at the University of Business and Economics in Vienna. She gained experience and knowledge while working in different corporate jobs and in the non-profit sector. She got in touch with the practice of yoga at the age of 20 with the wish to gain more flexibility. At 25, she was diagnosed with Hashimoto, an autoimmune disease of the thyroid. This disease made her question the stressful life she lived and forced her to slow down and reflect. She refused to believe in the idea of having to take hormonal medication for her entire life and dedicated her time to finding holistic solutions. She started diving deeper into the philosophy of yoga and found her passion and healing in meditation. After that, she learned through various courses about the power of plant medicine and completed courses in aromatherapy, Ayurveda, and yoga. She managed to heal her autoimmune disease and also her PMS. Out of her healing, she started creating artwork related to feminine energy, sexuality, and our connection to nature and planets.

She works with aromatherapy and chakra healing, combining different tools from yoga, embodiment, meditation, and the knowledge of plant medicine.

She is currently studying psychotherapy to understand the functions and interconnections between our physical, mental, and spiritual states. Her biggest wish is to use her own experience, knowledge, and healing to guide others through their processes in a holistic and sustainable way.

Website: www.risingroots.at

Instagram: the.common.mind

            the.rising.roots

Facebook: Theodora Elena Engelhart

CHAPTER 19

UNPACKING A LIFE

CREATING RITUALS TO SAY GOODBYE

Kendall Williams

MY STORY

We all know what death is and what it means.

For most of us, these are just stories detached from us and happening to someone else; many of us haven't faced the emotional and physical experience of the dying process. We may have had a relative or someone we know die and attended a funeral, sent flowers or a card to express our condolences, but we still have a sense of disconnection about what the dying process is. We feel uncomfortable talking about our mortality or considering that death will come to us or someone close to us one day. Conversations about death are swept under the carpet, or subjects are changed quickly, all in fear of upsetting someone or creating a negative and depressing mood. Within our happiness-focused culture, we're encouraged to celebrate the now, aim towards life goals and achievements ahead.

From the moment you're born, you've been taught and encouraged to celebrate achievements and milestones such as birthdays, graduations, new jobs, engagements, marriages, new babies, and anniversaries, to just name a few. All these beautiful occasions have rituals and ceremonies to embrace life; they express community, connection, and celebration. We understand what purpose these celebrations represent in our life, how to celebrate the occasion, what's expected of us, and how to behave within society's expectations. Think of how many life events you've attended or created so far, and how much experience you've gained. Experiencing these events firsthand has created comfort and knowledge within you of what to do, how to feel, and what role you play in each occasion.

Death often catches us by surprise or sneaks up slowly in our life, and we fall deep into the experience before we have had a chance to catch our breath. Finding yourself at that moment without a road map, experience, or knowledge of what to do, how to feel, or which role you should play, you realize that nobody taught you about dying. Nobody taught you how to unpack a life and say goodbye. What comes before a funeral, and how do you navigate that time? How do you move through the shock of your life-changing forever? Many of us feel helpless as we stand on the sidelines of the dying process, uncertain of what to do. How do we assist the person going through the death process—their family, friends, and ourselves— with the tide of emotions rising with every tick of the clock?

I'm really passionate about my work in holistic healing specializing in Shamanic practice, focused on heart and soul work, helping others remove what is blocking their empowerment path, embrace fears, and reset the life path. Before we relocated, I ran a successful practice, volunteered once a week at a local hospice, and juggled being a wife and Mumma bear of two kids. I was blessed that the hospice I helped was open-minded about energy work and had a volunteer reiki team. I joined the team and loved it. Hands-on energy work is one of the most powerful tools you can use in the dying process, and I learned a lot of the physical aspects and signs to be aware of as the body breaks down to complete the death journey. I experienced many different types of conditions: cancer, organ failure, old age, tumors, and blindness. I addressed different states of consciousness, communication issues, and other ailments that occur when the physical self begins to change during the dying process. Our focus as volunteer energy workers was to assist each person and their family to find calm in a stressful situation, and support with love, kindness, and compassion. We were also there to assist and give healings to the staff, who to this day, I believe, should be the most celebrated in our society.

It was here I met so many families and witnessed their experiences. Rarely did I see family or friends that knew how to navigate the death experience. It was like every room was a different TV show; some rooms were angry and uncertain, some serene and peaceful, and others felt helpless waiting for their loved one to die. People often didn't know how to act or what was required of them. Love was always present, but the lack of experience or understanding of what to do or how to contribute often caused relationships to become strained and uncomfortable, as extreme emotions would arise between family members. Everyone was just trying to find solid ground while dealing with feelings of guilt, overwhelm, confusion, the pressure of unsaid words, and old relationship patterns surfacing and in need of healing.

There was also the denial of accepting the death process, the fear of what was next, and accepting and letting go of a loved one. Feelings of helplessness were fueled when realizing their loved one was dying and didn't need anything anymore in a conventional sense. Gifts, food, parties, or flowers, all the items we're so familiar with giving when we come together to acknowledge life's milestones, seemed suddenly useless and unnecessary.

I'm forever grateful I had this experience and training in my life; it changed my understanding of death and gave me the gift of 'no-regrets living.' I also acknowledge that as a volunteer, I could support and connect with all those I met, but I was part of the external experience for them. I left the hospice eighteen months after joining the energy worker's team; we had decided to leave the Gold Coast and move back to Sydney to be closer to family. Only a year after this move, I would go through such a personal experience with the death of a friend and understand on a deeper level how hard it is to let go and the fear and challenges that arise on the path to a peaceful passing.

Like all big moves, it required new schools, making new friends, and starting all over again. We settled in pretty quickly having pre-school aged kids and knew from experience the best way to make friends was to get to know other parents, which usually depended on which kids your kids clicked with at school. After unpacking, we launched our new life into play dates, awkward conversations, and cups of tea on the path to finding our tribe again. I truly believe every person in your life has a divine purpose, and when my daughter took a liking to a sweet little boy in her class, I had no idea where that path ahead would take us.

I met Fran through a group of mums at school, and they were all a hoot! Fran and I bonded because our kids took a shine to each other. Fran, like me, was a straight shooter. No time for anything but the truth, and to be honest, she was a bit standoffish with me in the beginning, but once we worked each other out, we made a bond. When I met Fran, she had been through breast cancer, a double mastectomy, chemo, and was on the road to recovery. She had a bullet-proof attitude and was getting on with life. Fran was a take-charge woman who ran her own business, was a wonderful mum of two kids, and happily married. I remember the day she phoned me to say her check-up was done, and she was given the all-clear and green lights all the way. How happy and relieved we all felt. We understood cancer was an ongoing journey, but this was our first big milestone, and we were ready to celebrate after all holding our collective breaths for good news. A couple of weeks later, her arm began to swell, and it was diagnosed as lymphedema, which is common when lymph glands are removed during breast cancer surgery. She was sent off for lymphatic drainage massages. The pain and swelling didn't subside, and we were off to the osteopath for realignment to help with that, but before we knew it, she was diagnosed with bone cancer in her arm as secondary cancer to the original breast cancer. We were devastated.

Everything accelerated and happened so fast, doctors seemed to be scrambling to work out a plan, and our beautiful friend was clearly distressed as the shock settled in around us. She went from weeks of hospital treatment and painful radiation to being sent home and classified as a palliative care patient. In such a short space of time, her world literally fell apart as she was given a best-case scenario of 18 months.

The shock she and her family endured over this time was extreme, and if it weren't for her best friend's love and nerves of steel, navigating these moments and taking the next steps would have been impossible. This is where I learned the first tool in coping with the death process. Everyone needs a purpose, a purpose that plays to their strengths. Fran's best friend Dani was a fantastic coordinator, and she knew what Fran needed. She didn't have a problem with paperwork, speaking up, asking questions, or saying no to anyone if it went against Fran's wishes. She also understood what she wasn't, so we quickly built a small tight team (The Inner Team) to reduce the chaos, create purpose for others, and support the most important person, the person passing, to have a good death. Death was coming whether we liked it or not. Dani stepped into the role as The Voice (Defender of Wishes, Paperwork, Family Coordinator, Palliative Care Admin).

I stepped into the role of Confidante (Heart Healer, Emotional Support, Unpacking, Ceremonies), and we would often laugh about me being labeled in the hospice as her spiritual advisor. Fran wasn't deeply religious and had worked with me on her heart and spiritual blocks previously. She was scared and overwhelmed with the reality of dying and struggled most with letting go of her husband and kids. I couldn't even fathom being in her position and preparing to say goodbye to your children. Our kids were the same age, and we were also the same age. Thoughts would creep into my mind, and in many ways, she was my mirror. I would question: *If this were me, how would I cope?* I felt I wouldn't have been able to accept that diagnosis either, which honestly triggered a lot of fear and panic. *How on earth was I going to be able to support her?* Many of us turn away from helping because of our internal struggle. You feel fear, guilt, and helplessness, but this is where the tool of purpose creates structure and magic. For me, heart work, unpacking emotions, breaking down blocks, and coaching are my passion, and just like her best friend Dani, I had to embrace what I did well and bring it to the table. Your purpose then replaces fear, and you can be of service again.

In my work, one of the greatest Shamanic tools of practice is the art of delabeling and letting go of our roles in life to bring peace and the deep knowing that we are eternal beings. The Tibetan practice of living and dying teaches us that to die well; we must pass without attachment and let go of holding on tight to our current life. The one thing that connects us as humans, no matter the culture or belief system, is ceremony and ritual. To help Fran, I quickly realized she had to close those doorways, roles, and attachments she'd built in her life, and we would need to create moments, conversations, ceremonies, and actions to find that peace within and let go.

My role as Confidante required taking each day as a new moment and opportunity to release what was coming up for Fran. It required listening and allowing her to be heard in private without fear of upsetting anyone, and focusing on clearing fear or regrets and feelings of missed opportunities in life. It required laughing and celebrating the fun memories and interacting with the real her, without sadness or pity of someone sick or dying. The reality is, dying is uncomfortable. Some days she was angry, in pain, or cranky, and allowing her to work through these moments and not taking it personally was a gift for us both. Those moments we had together and holding space for each other created so much healing.

One day I was spending time with her when her sweet, sensitive husband arrived. He took on the role of Care Giver (Fill in Family, Friends, Care for Kids, Work/Money, Hold the Fort at Home), but he found being at the hospice very challenging and confronting. Seeing your life partner go through this process was unbearable in many ways. We all cope differently, and we need to acknowledge the honesty in this. That morning it bothered Fran that her rings had become so loose she couldn't keep wearing them. As soon as she saw her husband, she thrust the rings out to him and said in a terse tone, "Here, take these home. I don't want to lose them, and you will need to keep them safe to give to our daughter." I could feel his discomfort and her emotion at that moment being stuffed down. I realized they originally put on these rings with so much love, ceremony, promises of the future, and celebration of a wedding, a door that needed to be closed. With the simplicity of creating a moment of ceremony and heart space, I took the rings from her and explained that you spoke your vows when you exchanged these rings, let's do that again now, in giving them back. I guided them through remembering that moment and speaking from their hearts as they exchanged rings back to close that door. It was raw, beautiful, honest, and filled with tears. So much healing happened at that moment; I will remember it forever.

Ceremonies do not have to be complicated or elaborate. They are about unpacking the roles and purpose of the experiences you have built on your earth walk, so you can let go. Not of the memories and wonder you created over your lifetime, but any pain, regret, unsaid moments, or fear of an incomplete life.

My beautiful, brave Fran passed peacefully in her sleep without fear of an incomplete life, under the light of a full moon with her husband by her side. Dani and I kissed her goodnight as usual, and I knew it was goodbye. It may seem strange, but I felt filled with joy that night. I could feel how at peace she was. We would grieve deeply later, but for now, we assisted her in the most important transition we make, going home to the stars. I feel her presence with me always. It was a privilege and a gift to be part of the journey with her, and the experience changed my life forever.

THE TOOL

Symptoms Arising for Person Dying, Caregivers, Friends, Family:

- Feeling helpless or useless
- Feeling scared, panic, anxiety, fear of the unknown
- Feeling like this isn't happening; disconnection or denial
- Not coping; feeling overwhelmed, scattered
- Extreme emotions or blame coming up; anger, sadness, guilt
- Feeling fractured
- Feeling unheard
- Feeling fearful of dying and letting go

Tool 1 - Creating the Inner Team Roles: Purpose and Planning

- The Voice (Defender of Wishes, Paperwork, Palliative Care Admin)
- The Confidante (Healer, Emotional Support, Unpacking, Ceremonies)
- The Provider (Supplies, Food, Items needed)
- The Care Giver (Fill in Family/Friends, Care for Kids, Money/Provider, Hold the Fort at Home)

Tool 2 - Unpacking: Ceremonies, Rituals, and Closing doors

Look at the roles the person passing needs to let go of. What are their fears regarding letting go? Create conversations, small ceremonies, and actions to help them close doors and unpack their life.

- Ceremony: Exchanging vows /rings; unpacking marriage
- Creating future letters, birthday cards for children, milestones
- Creating a video goodbye, letter, or message to be read after you pass
- Creating time to say goodbye to the special people in your life
- Being able to say no to seeing everyone
- Conversations of disappointment or regrets that you're holding back
- Conversations of anger and disbelief that this is happening to you

- Conversations of fears of responsibilities. Who will manage your roles when you pass?
- Conversations of fear of death or the dying process
- Conversations and choices of your funeral
- Ceremony: Last wishes; seeing the ocean, going outside, watching the sunrise
- Ceremony: Pre-funeral goodbye events

Kendall is a dynamic Shamanic practitioner and trainer. She is devoted to educating the benefits of connecting us back to our Shamanic roots and heart power. Her powerful sessions and teachings wake us up from modern-day stress, illness, and disempowerment, empowering us to tap into our unique medicine to heal ourselves. She creates permission to unfold the shadow emotions you may deny, helping you let go and find clarity in your life, clearing your way back to happiness, and realigning a powerful wellness path ahead.

Being an Empath, Kendall learned that growing up in Western culture as an Empath and experiencing disconnection, pressure, and the exhaustion of modern society deeply affects both our emotional and mental health. Kendall began a wellness journey to reclaim both her spiritual and emotional wellbeing. Her ongoing journey to wellness fires her passion for helping others and creating a Tribe of Love, Compassion, and Realignment in Western Culture.

Kendall runs the successful private practice Heart Hive and is also a partner in Earth Retreats on the Gold Coast, Australia.

For more information regarding private Shamanic Sessions or Shamanic Training events, contact Kendall at www.hearthive.com.au or email info@hearthive.com.au

Follow Kendall:

https://www.facebook.com/kendallhearthive/

https://www.instagram.com/heart.hive/

https://www.facebook.com/earthretreats

https://www.instagram.com/earth_retreats/

CHAPTER 20

INTUITION

COMPLETION THROUGH LISTENING TO YOUR HIGHER SELF

Melissa McGlone, Healing Artist of Metaphysical Modalities

MY STORY

Experiencing death came early in my life; I was just eight years old when my mother died very tragically and unexpectedly. The product of dysfunction and long-term sexual abuse, my mother lived a hard and tortured life being diagnosed with schizophrenia as a teenager. Likely the culmination of the abuse and a genetic predisposition, the fact she functioned as well as she did was nothing less than miraculous.

Suffice it to say, I didn't know my mother well as her care for me and my brother and sister was understandably sporadic at best. My siblings and I, in turn, became a product of the social system when our alcoholic father surrendered his role as a parent and signed us over to be wards of the court of the Commonwealth of Virginia. Fortunately for me, I was often cared for by my maternal grandmother as an infant and eventually fostered by a great-aunt and uncle who would become, for all intents and purposes, my parents.

My mother's mission in life was always to work hard and provide for my siblings and me to the best of her ability. When she was well and even when she was sick, this drive had so much momentum and passion behind it that people around her were often surprised and dismayed at what she could accomplish. She was a genius, and her work ethic stellar; she never had an issue finding employment. Sadly, her bouts with breaks in reality came too often. When fighting the disease, she would also fight the medicine intended to keep her well. This became what must've been an exhausting merry-go-round of sickness to wellness and back again. Through it all, however, she never surrendered.

She finally found some peace when she met her second husband and soul-mate during an extended period of wellness. The fast and furious fairy-tale romance led to, once again, my mother wanting to gather her ducklings. The couple wed and followed their dream of settling on the West Coast in San Francisco. It wouldn't be long before her long-term dream would be fulfilled and she could have her entire family together.

Shortly after finally acquiring some extended balance and happiness in her life, one night in the throes of a severe episode of pain, she tragically overdosed on some of her medication. I do not believe my mother did this purposefully. In my family, this horrible series of events is still shrouded in mystery and misunderstanding, to which we all do not agree. I happen to align on the subject with my aunt, my mother's middle sister, and best friend. With everything she was working towards and living for, there was no way this was the time or place to end it all.

I was under the care of my great-aunt and uncle when my mother died. I'll never forget my great-aunt taking the phone call and delivering the sobering news, her almost faint-like stance bracing herself against the wall and shielding her eyes as if to block the sun. She could barely whisper the words, "your mother has died."

The burial of my mother was perplexing for me. As my step-grandfather placed the small gold rectangle box in the hole in the ground, none of it made much sense. I had been to funerals before, but never like this. This was something different altogether. I was in third grade at the time, and I would then just be learning about cremation. My elementary school teacher shared with me much later that I came back to school begging many questions. "What happens after you die? What happens to your body when it's cremated?" Apparently, lots of inquiry into the biology of what happens after death.

So here I found myself after my mother's death in the loving arms of my great-aunt, a devoted kindergarten teacher, and child-lover, and my great-uncle, a hard-working jack of many trades and later retiree spending most of his days walking the dog and playing golf as his "job." I was safe here. I felt loved and cared for and, so much so, my aunt's and uncle's belief systems definitely became part of my own. I grew up with good, sturdy, old-school values, and part of that influence was the solid belief in God and something beyond the physical plane.

My great-aunt, Naomi, was an enthusiastic follower of the late, great Edgar Cayce. Known in his time as *The Sleeping Prophet*, Cayce was also regarded as the father of holistic medicine by *The Journal of the American Medical Association*. Books by Edgar Cayce and other psychics like Jeane Dixon and Sylvia Browne furnished her bookshelves. Esoteric poets like Khalil Gibran and his books, especially *The Prophet*, were one of her big influences. She most assuredly believed in reincarnation.

Naomi was fascinated with the occult, but like Edgar Cayce, was a devout Christian. Although I was baptized Catholic, I was raised in the more moderate but high Episcopal Church and also consider myself Christian. My spirituality would come later as it naturally evolved over time. Little did I know as a child, my aunt's influence would one day become a center point of my own healing journey and life's work.

Edgar Cayce, being a household name, I grew up thinking this was all, of course, natural. The supernatural being the norm for me. I remember hearing my aunt having hush-hush conversations in whispers with her sister-in-law Carrie, who she thought of and trusted as a sister. Late night chats about out-of-body experiences, prophetic dreams, and my aunt's "jingles," as she would call them, were what I now know to be channeled writings. Oh, how fortunate I was to be privy to such secrets and mysteries! These impressions really shaped me and made me open-minded to all things metaphysical. Perhaps even an open channel, shall we say, that would later be discovered and nurtured.

The first time I recall a "knowing" was at a Halloween party at my church. Halloween was a big deal to my kindergarten teacher aunt, and it was to me too. This particular year, my costume was the washerwoman from *The Carol Burnett Show*. I have to say I was totally cute, dimples and washerwoman hat and clunky stadium boots and apron and mop and all. My best friend Tina and I got to the party early, and when we arrived, one of the party arrangers was steadily placing candy corn, piece by piece, into a big jar. We would later find out one of the party games was "guess how many pieces of candy corn" to win a prize. Whoever was closest to the number would be the winner. 763. That's the number that came into my head, so that was my guess. Sure enough, the winning number was exactly 763, right on the money. I think they must've thought I cheated somehow; I know differently.

In my twenties, I was venturing out for the weekend to the mountains with my dear friend Becky. We were headed to our beloved Shrinemont, an Episcopal retreat center, with our church family. We were in no hurry, just enjoying the autumn weather and the winding (but treacherous) mountain road. Almost to our destination, a big semi-truck came up behind us. The truck didn't bother me in the least, but I soon said to Becky, "I'm just going to pull over and let him pass." As he whizzed by, we exchanged honks and continued on our way. Suddenly, some large piece of machinery came barreling out the back of his rig, and he zoomed ahead. When we reached him, his rig was up a runaway ramp. Clearly shaken, he said, "Ma'am, I'm glad you pulled over, I just lost my brakes."

Unacknowledged, intuition took the forefront in my life. My own clairaudience had to be pointed out to me. I was having coffee with my friends Carlos and Jesse, who are healers themselves, when Jesse said, "Did you know you are channeling right now?" "Really?" I responded. I giggled like a child who had just discovered how to whistle. We all smiled and laughed about it, and it just *was*.

I was very connected to my mother's sister Cindy, who was the life-of-the-party and had a sparkly, dynamic personality. She thought of me as a daughter, and her son became a brother. Later in life, she would have a daughter, but in the meantime, we filled gaps for each other, she wanting to experience a daughter and me desperately needing a mother. The impact she had on my life was tremendous. Cindy was an amazing mother and taught me so much.

She lived to the fullest even after being diagnosed with cancer. One Mother's Day weekend, she anxiously summoned her children and me to the beach where she lived. Whatever the news, it didn't sound good. I planned my trip, sensing the urgency; I would've done anything in my power for her. The feeling it was imperative for me to go could not be denied.

We gathered at her favorite restaurant and enjoyed a lovely Mother's Day brunch. This special time together will always be a standout, and I was honored to be included. She wanted to take a walk on the beach after brunch, perhaps grounding herself in one of her favorite places to be able to deliver the news. We walked through the sand, and she began to become emotional. She delivered the news she so desperately needed to be unburdened from. The cancer was back and not treatable. I don't recall how much time she told us she had. One year? Two years? Not enough. Never enough. We cried together and tried to comfort each other. She was brave. I believe that was the beginning of us never being the same. Change. It was coming. We would never be the same.

The months that followed were not easy for my aunt. It was a day-by-day process, many bad with less and less frequent good days. My visits were emotionally hard on her and perhaps selfish on my part. I didn't want to let her go; of course, none of us did. She was understandably afraid, and she wasn't sure how long she could keep going. She was placed in at-home palliative care.

I got the call from my cousin one autumn Saturday morning. "If you want to be there, come now." This Saturday was different than my typical full day of clients. I was ending at 12:00 pm, very unusually. At a moment's notice, I ran home and quickly packed a bag. I was on the road within the hour.

I arrived at the hospital in the late afternoon and sprinted to her room. A sign saying "peace" with a dove on it was prominent on the doorknob; I can still see it so clearly in my mind's eye. Inside everyone was there. My cousins, significant others, my aunt's companion. Everyone. I was the last piece of the puzzle, so it seemed. My cousins were keeping vigil over my auntie. She waited for me, and deep down, I knew it.

As I watched my aunt, unconscious and breathing, I realized I hadn't phoned home to let anyone know I had arrived safely. I left the room to make my call, passing some children's drawings on my way to the lobby. The crayon drawings of a Native American grandmother, mother, and child seemed so poignant, and I found solace in it in that moment.

I proceeded to ring my new boyfriend; we had just met that previous May. We were in love, and although the relationship was just in the budding stage, I was leaning heavily on him for comfort. Shortly through our conversation as we spoke, something welled up inside of me. This tidal wave of terror making my body temperature quickly rise. I was in a panic. What the heck was I doing? I was frightened to my core, fearing I had just blown the whole plan. Without explanation and mid-sentence, I abruptly cut the conversation short, said my goodbyes, and raced back to the hospital room.

Entering the hospital room for the second time, something *felt* different. Everyone was asleep this time. Adrenalin pumping through my veins, I, on the other hand, not having days of sleeplessness, was more than wide awake. I could see my aunt was still breathing. *Oh, thank God*, I thought. Then something quickly shifted. I could literally feel it in my body. Something changed in my aunt's breath. It was subtle yet painfully clear to me she was about to take her last breath. "John, David, John, David, wake up; I think it's time." We all gathered around her. We were all there: her son, her daughter, her long-time companion, me, her niece-daughter. It was just as she wanted it. As she inhaled and exhaled her last three breaths, we were honored to be there to witness it.

After her death, when everyone had a chance to say their goodbyes, my cousins were getting ready to head home after days of sleep deprivation. I said to my cousin, "Would you be okay if I stayed with her a bit longer?" "Yes," he replied. "Just don't do anything weird to the body." I did not take offense to this, as I suppose my cousin knows me better than most. I didn't plan to do anything ritualistic to the body; I just wanted to stay with her as long as I could. What popped into my head was to download the Beatles' song *Let It Be*. I played the song as the nurses prepared her, and it continued to play as I took my last sobering walk with my beloved aunt. The nurses graciously let me stay with her to the very last moment. As I walked away from my aunt in the physical for the last time, I felt complete. My life would never be the same and certainly would not be for my cousins. But she died as she lived, with those around her she loved most and who loved her most. She wouldn't have had it any other way. I was present to how grateful I was to have experienced a mother's true, endearing, and unconditional love. Her boundless generosity of self and limitless love still astounds me to this day, so many years later.

THE TOOL

The tool that has helped me in honoring someone in the death process is intuition. I believe this tool can be used by anyone who chooses to honor it, as in my opinion, everyone has in their possession some amount of metaphysical gifts. They may be unacknowledged as mine were, unused, dormant, or denied, but I do believe we as spiritual beings, of course, have these special tools.

As weaved throughout my story, I've given various examples of how intuition has benefited my life. The most pertinent example is how my intuition saved me from missing my beloved aunt's death process. Perhaps review moments in your life where you used your own intuition for your greater good without you even realizing it. I bet you can think of one, if not several. When you think of an example, try to get yourself present to how you felt when you had the intuitive thought which prompted you to take (or not take) an action. Were you panicked? Frightened? Were you happy or joyful? Did you feel a pit inside of your stomach? Were you nervous or scared? My advice would be to follow the strong emotion, whether positive or negative. Use that as your map, your guide.

When witnessing someone as they pass, I believe they get to decide who they want in the room on some level—honor that. Check in with yourself and ask yourself: Am I acting with their highest good in mind or mine? The signs and symbols will be there for you if you trust. I believe intuition is a tool that can be well-applied in assisting someone in the death process.

So listen to that voice, that intuitive gift inside of you. That voice that says, "Call your mother" or "make that trip" or "tell them you love them;" tune in. You can use this gift too; it's there for you.

Melissa's healing journey began when she was diagnosed with chronic endometriosis and was deemed infertile. Her determination to heal the disease naturally led her to embark on a 90-day raw food detoxification program. Shortly after completing the program, Melissa became pregnant with her daughter and delivered her second child, a son, two years later.

Her life's work became a commitment to helping others heal, and she became certified in Colon Hydrotherapy through the Edgar Cayce/Reilly School of Massotherapy in Virginia Beach. She is currently advanced level certified through the International Association for Colon Hydrotherapy and sat for their National Board.

With 20-years of experience, she has enhanced her practice with other forms of detox, nutritional coaching, and intuitive readings. She recently launched her new product and coaching business, *The Goddess Mother Healing Box* www.goddessmotherhealing.com wanting to share her miraculous story to inspire others that they too can heal.

CHAPTER 21

GRIEVING OUT LOUD WHEN THERE ARE NO WORDS

HOW WRITING ABOUT THE LOSS OF MY CHILD HELPED ME HEAL

Shelley Sake

MY STORY

We all know them—the unfortunate families who suffer the sudden loss of a child. They're the families we feel awkward talking to because we feel we don't have the right words to comfort them. The normal platitudes seem all wrong because the natural order of things has been upset. We feel terrible, but we avoid them. Acting "normal" around them is so difficult for us that we sometimes slowly and unintentionally remove ourselves from their lives, wishing them the best but not able to relate to what they're going through. We wish we knew how to help but are, at the same time, not wanting to add to their pain. I know this is true because I know those families, too. I knew them long before we became one of them.

I became an angel mom on a beautiful September evening in Minnesota. As far as the day goes, it was nothing out of the ordinary. Our identical twin daughters, Abby and Maddy, completed just their second day as juniors in high school that day. They came home together, as always, full of chatter about the new year, friends, and their plans. Maddy agreed to help out over the dinner hour at her part-time job at a barbecue restaurant, so after some homework and an early dinner, she changed and left. I remember saying, "I love you. See you later." as she headed out the door. I'm grateful to this day that those were my final words to her, because it was not long before she was gone. Forever.

Maddy finished her short shift early and sent a text asking if she could run out to check on a friend's progress on the truck he was working on. This wasn't unusual. Maddy was a gregarious girl with a lot of friends who loved the country life. She and Abby's social life consisted of lots of bonfires, four-wheeling,, and really, anything "country." She planned to be home by 8:30, so I agreed. As it turns out, she arrived at her friend's home a short distance out of town, only to find he had gone to town for parts. Not one to sit still long, Maddy texted me that she was on her way home. As she left her friend's house to drive home, she moved over slightly at the crest of a hill to make way for a man walking his dog and was in a head-on collision with the very friend she had gone to visit.

It's funny what I remember about the next few hours. I remember my husband, Mike's sharp intake of breath after answering the phone. I knew instantly it was bad news. A sheriff called to tell us about the accident and to let us know she was being airlifted to Regions Hospital in St. Paul, the nearest level 1 trauma center. He told Mike that we should hurry, that Maddy had significant injuries to her legs, but that she was expected to survive. I remember what I wore and the decision to drive separately should one of us need to stay overnight. I remember that Abby insisted on taking a blanket that my mom had made for Maddy "in case she needed something from home." I remember calling our oldest daughter at college and telling her she didn't have to come home but that we'd keep her posted on Maddy's condition. I can't remember if I actually did that.

We arrived in the ER to hear that Maddy was conscious upon arrival, knew her name and that two surgeons were called to prepare for surgery on her legs. In the meantime, however, her blood pressure dropped, and they took her to surgery out of concern for internal injuries. As word trickled out, friends and family started to gather in the waiting room with us and in the lobby of the hospital. After one update around 11:00 pm, a nurse finally came out and asked Mike, Abby, and me to follow her. In a smaller waiting room, a surgeon informed us that Maddy had not survived her injuries. There truly are no words to describe what it's like to hear that your child has died; it's the most physical pain I have ever felt, followed only by seeing Abby's reaction to the loss of her twin and then having to tell Alyssa, who had just arrived in the waiting room.

We were able to see Maddy before leaving the hospital that night. I struggled to stay long as the finality of what we were facing started to sink in. While Maddy looked herself, it was clear that our pretty, cheerful, and bubbly girl was too pale and too still. My mind could not stop willing her to wake up, but it was obvious that was not going to happen. She would never come home again. I remember a nurse handing me the ponytail holders Maddy wore around her wrist and the rings she had on her fingers. I will never forget walking to my car, knowing that we left Maddy there alone. That particular memory will haunt me for a lifetime.

What followed were some of the most agonizing days of my life. While we were a family blessed with wonderful family and friends, I found that I mostly wanted to be alone to focus on my husband and my girls. My daughter's accident was on every Minneapolis and St. Paul television station, and we had reporters at our door asking for comments. We declined all of them. There was nothing to say. Instead, we walked through the difficult things with the help of family and close friends. Picking the clothes Maddy would wear, selecting her plot at the cemetery, and planning her service were all we could manage.

Through everything, Maddy's friends are what I believe kept me going in the early days. I was grateful to them for keeping Maddy present, and I felt responsible for their healing. They were a wonderful bunch of kids who loved our girl, and they were hurting so badly. They sold t-shirts and bracelets, made posters, got tattoos, visited us, held vigils at the crash site, wore her favorite purple, and planned a huge caravan on the day of her funeral with all those loud trucks she loved so much. It was over 100 vehicles long with windows painted, horns honking, and music blaring. Maddy would have loved it.

We also had the humbling experience of realizing that we didn't know everything about Maddy. We received letters from kids who Maddy helped through difficult things they were facing and letters describing what a good friend, student, and coworker she was. Plus, she was a ton of fun, a big personality in a petite little body. Known to be a bit of a chatterbox, Maddy wasn't one to stay quiet about anything. Had I really thought about it, she showed me the answer to healing all along. Do it out loud.

In those early days of loss, I felt completely overwhelmed with both grief and gratitude. I longed to share my feelings with others but found it incredibly painful to do face to face. The fact was that few knew what it was like to be in our shoes, but I desperately needed them to understand.

In the end, I turned to the one thing that always came easy for me—writing.

THE TOOL

I'm not an expert in healing, but I know with certainty that our culture has it wrong. Who hasn't heard, "she's changed," or "we don't see him anymore?" There is a reason for that; the grieving know how uncomfortable we make others feel and too often try to get back to "normal" for them. So, we mask our pain, push it down, and delay or completely avoid dealing with it. People who care about you yearn for the "old you" to come back. When they realize that won't happen, it becomes awkward. It's a sad fact that people become isolated, and some even turn to self-harm in a variety of forms. Here's the deal; like it or not, you have to go through grief. You don't get to fast forward and skip the hard parts.

I'm a social person with a large group of friends but seeing *them* in person and seeing them hurt was very hard for me. I wanted them, as well as family and Maddy's friends, to know what I was going through. Grief is exhausting, so I chose social media as my vehicle for the sake of efficiency. I could reach a lot of people quickly. I definitely over-shared and was probably criticized by some, but I didn't care. You shouldn't either. Don't let others judge your healing journey. The relief I felt after writing from my heart was cathartic, but the support I received in response canceled my self-talk and made me realize how many people were hurting for me and with me. You will form an army of loving supporters, and you will come to learn that many never tire of helping. *Put it out there.*

When you lose a child or someone close to you unexpectedly, your life is forever altered. You may not realize it, but when you wake in the morning, you unconsciously think about each of your kids, your spouse, and those closest to you. That doesn't change when one of them dies, and you need a place to put those feelings in that moment. *Write them down.*

You will have times that you have no choice but to accept the kindness of others. There may be meals brought to you, tasks done for you, benefits planned for you, dedications given in your loved ones' memory, or big and small gifts given in remembrance of that person. The kindness can be overwhelming. You will be humbled and feel incapable of ever repaying the kindness shown. *Share what it means to you.*

I recommend trying many "tools" in your healing journey. Some will work, and some will not. For me, it was therapy, my angel mom's group, and writing. You will get suggestions from many places—your church, your doctor, your friends, and from strangers. Try them all, and remember that it may be a combination of things that help. Tell people what works and what doesn't and why. By sharing, you'll tell them what you need and give them ideas for how to help. Your suggestions could also help them now or in the future. *Fill your toolbox and share your tools.*

There will be hard days. Your loved ones' birthday and their angel anniversary, of course, but also all the "should have been here" moments of graduation, showers, weddings, and funerals. Old traditions could feel wrong with someone missing. It's okay and healthy to create new traditions. It may upset people when you do, so tell them why you need to do it. If they don't understand, it's because they're thinking of themselves but not allowing you to do the same exact thing. There are days you will hear a song your loved one liked, see their favorite cereal at the grocery store, or see a gift that would have been perfect for them. Those instances can bring you to tears, and that is completely normal. Life does move on for others, even when you can't, and you will hurt because of it. You'll start to feel like your healing is taking too long. It's important to understand that grief and healing are a process that can't be rushed. *There is no timeline for grief.*

There will be signs. Write about them. It's the personal nature of the sign and the timing that will convince you. You'll be surprised how many others experience them and long to share them. Give them a voice. When someone tells you they don't believe in them, let them know it's because they haven't experienced one. I always tell people I'm just as sure of them as they are unsure of them. Signs are healing moments, and for many, proof our loved one is still near to us, guiding us and comforting us. Who cares if others don't believe? It's what you experience that counts. *Never be afraid to tell your story.*

Your friends and family will share your words because it will make them feel and understand something new. You will meet empathetic people and form life-long friendships with complete strangers. With those new friends, you can share what commercials you can no longer watch, the fears you have now that you didn't before, and how sometimes others are cruel without intending to be. They will give you unbiased feedback and support. They will help you heal in unexpected ways and validate you. Life is hard, and losses come in many forms. They will make you feel sane on days sanity seems far away. Let them in. These helpers will share the tools that work for them and give you advice. In return, you will become a resource for them, and that will give you purpose. *Widen your audience.*

Share how you plan to honor your loved one and allow others to participate. We have an annual scholarship in Maddy's name that goes to a local high school student who reminds us most of Maddy. A group of my friends organized a fundraiser, and our family provides a match annually from that fund. We have also started the Maddy's Smile Project on Facebook. Maddy had an infectious smile and a love of surprises, so it's simply a pay-it-forward movement where we invite others to spread kindness and fun. Others do golf outings, annual hunting or baking events, fundraisers for causes that were important to them, or organized volunteer activities. Pick something that reminds you of your loved one, and write about it. *Bring a legacy to light.*

I believe grieving is hard work and a life-long commitment. Don't try to accomplish it unarmed and alone. The act of healing requires an evolution. How you evolve is up to you; embrace bitterness, hurt, and anger or embrace hope, love, and legacy. Start accumulating tools and use them whenever you need them. Writing out loud is one simple tool that will allow people in your life to walk alongside you and understand your journey. It is also a powerful tool that will allow you to release your pain a little at a time while giving you the opportunity to build a legacy of helping others.

Shelley Sake is married to her husband of 32 years, Mike, and is the mother of three daughters—Alyssa, and identical twins, Abby and Maddy. Maddy gained her wings on September 6, 2012, in a car accident near her hometown of Hastings, MN. Shelley is also a mother-in-law to Jesse and a brand new grandma to Savannah Rose, who shares her middle name with her aunt Maddy. Shelley is a marketing professional and the founder of the Maddy's Smile Project on Facebook, which is open for anyone to join. She is in the process of writing her first full-length book..

CHAPTER 22

THE POWER OF HEALING TOUCH

USING TOUCH IN END OF LIFE CARE

Dr. Jennifer Browne, DPT

MY STORY

I had the honor and privilege of being present when both my grandmother and my grandmother-in-law took their last breath and peacefully crossed to the other side. I learned many lessons from these experiences. With each passing, I've learned that we hold in our hands the power of touch. This simple tool can provide comfort and reassurance to help our loved ones in their time of transition.

Grandmother

We decided that hospice was the way to go. My grandmother lived a long life, and her battle with congestive heart failure was almost over. She was in and out of the hospital over the previous year and, at one point, admitted to a skilled nursing facility to undergo rehabilitation. My grandmother was never much of an exerciser, and she didn't like to be away from home or under the care of so many unfamiliar faces. She wanted to be at home when she died, and as a family, we all supported that decision. We met with the admitting nurse to hospice and were able to complete a plan of care for my grandmother that included her wishes and desires for end-of-life care.

The next day a nice man came to play some music and sit with my grandma. We were all very happy to see she was receiving such great care. Over the next several days, many different nurses, musicians, church members, family, and sitters came to spend time with my grandma. Eventually, she began to have more difficulty breathing and with mobility, and the swelling in her legs started to cause her pain. My mother and I were given direction from her hospice nurse, "I'm going to show you how to start administering sublingual morphine when she's in pain." Her pain was increasing, and the anxiety associated with increased difficulty breathing as her body began to fill up with fluid from the congestive heart failure was progressively getting worse.

My grandmother was eventually confined to a hospital bed in her bedroom and was on continuous oxygen. No longer able to walk and come into her den where she could see her beautiful garden and the many varieties of birds that frequented her garden, my mother and I began taking turns staying with her in her room. At this point in the process, I started to feel anxious. Although we had lost several members of our family, I was never present when they died. My father passed away suddenly. After arriving at the hospital to visit him, I approached the information desk and was informed he had passed away several hours before I arrived.

What would it be like to see someone take their last breath?

What would my sweet grandmother look like?

What would she say?

Would she be able to talk?

Would she be in pain?

These were some of the many questions swirling around in my head. In my 21 years as a physical therapist, my sole purpose has always been to help people improve their lives, to help people live out their best lives, even if that meant adapting the way they did things so they could maintain a better quality of life. However, here I was in a situation quite the opposite of what I was trained to do. What could I offer at this moment? What could I do that could be instrumental, comforting, and of help in a situation that seemed helpless to most?

Soon we were giving my grandmother morphine tablets more frequently as she continued to look increasingly uncomfortable and more agitated and restless. The night before she passed away, I was with her and could hear her calling out different names I didn't recognize. She would say, "look down there by the creek and go down the hill." That night my mother took the first watch. We had a chair in her room, and we would sit with her and keep a close eye on her for signs of discomfort. At this point, it was no longer a matter of if but when. If she started to get agitated or more fidgety, we would administer more morphine. I took a rest on the couch in the living room so I could take over for my mom when she got tired. I didn't sleep well and woke up sometime in the morning. I noticed that my mom did not come and get me to take over as we planned. "Mom, go get some rest. I'll watch over Grandma," I said. Just as my mom left the room, my grandma sat up with her eyes wide open and then laid back down crossways on the bed. Her breathing began to get very shallow and more frequent, and I knew I had to move her so she wouldn't fall off of the bed. As I took hold of her upper body to slide her shoulders over, I could tell she was about to take her last breath and called for my mom. "Mom, come quick!" Just before she came into the room, my grandmother took her last breath.

Grandmother-in-law

Several years later, I again had the privilege and honor to be present when a family member was called to cross over to the other side. This story is very similar to my grandmother's in many ways. The difference is that I discovered a tool I could use to help my grandmother during her last days that I had all along. Lillian, my husband's grandmother, was diagnosed with stage IV lung cancer that metastasized to her bone. She tried to fight it as best as she could. About six years before the metastasis, she successfully completed radiation therapy and safely said that she was in remission. When cancer came back to rear its ugly head, her body could not fight off the inevitable. She was a tough lady, and eventually, like my grandmother, she was unable to leave her bed, and the decision was made that hospice was the way to go. Many friends, church members, nurses, and family members were able to visit her while she was in hospice care. On the day she passed away, she called out different names of people I never heard of before early in the morning. Midday, she started to become restless, and I was considering starting the sublingual morphine to help reduce her anxiety and restlessness, just as I had done for my grandmother. At that moment, I sat next to her and held her hand, and stroked it gently. As I held her hand, I told her, "It's okay to let go. The family loves you very much."

Her hand was thin, motionless, and almost weightless. Her breathing became more shallow and frequent. I continued to hold her hand and reassure her by repeating the words that it was okay for her to go. I called my husband and told him that this was it, and just then, she took her last breath. I was there with her, and I will always remember that peaceful moment.

THE TOOL

Touch had a different meaning and purpose when I was using it as a physical therapist to help my patients walk, improve their range of motion, or help reduce pain. Using touch, and more specifically, gentle touch can help facilitate communication and provide comfort to those in the dying process.

What to do: Do not be afraid to gently place your hand on a person who is in the process of dying. Often when someone is dying, they can be in pain or feel scared, alone, or depressed. You can gently place your hand on their shoulder, back, arm, or hand. Often, the person may not be able to speak to you, hear you, or acknowledge you. They will, however, be able to feel your presence when you place your hand on them. This is an excellent way to communicate that you are there for that person. You do not have to touch the person for long. Imagine if that person were healthy and you came to greet them. Typically a quick handshake or hug will suffice. The touch you provide can be as quick as you like, or it can last longer. There were many times that I sat with my grandmother and held her hand while she lay asleep and prayed for her. I held her hand gently as I prayed and did not let go until I finished the prayer. If the person is not too frail and is willing, you can provide a gentle massage in large, slow-moving strokes across the back, arm, or legs.

The Benefits: A simple touch can provide reassurance and safety and contribute to an improvement in their overall well-being. Another benefit to touch is the transference of energy from one body to another. Later in my career, I was fortunate enough to learn Reiki and incorporate the tool into my practice. Reiki uses life energy that transfers from our hands to assist with reducing pain, anxiety, and depression. This transference of energy from me to my loved one can provide what is needed during end-of-life care. Reiki supports the whole person physically, emotionally, mentally, and spiritually. As I reflect on the times that I was present when both of my grandmothers passed, I can see the connection between the tools I have learned and the dying process. Touch can help with reducing restlessness, anxiety, pain, fear, depression, and loneliness. Overall, in the palms of your hands, you have the power to provide great comfort to a person undergoing a very difficult time in their life. Not only will the person you're touching feel more connected to you, but you'll feel more connected to them as well. I hope this tool will be helpful to you when having to provide comfort and support to someone in the process of dying.

Jennifer Browne, DPT, is a physical therapist who has been practicing for over 21 years. She lives in northern Virginia with her husband, daughter, and dog. She started her career at the Mayo Clinic in Rochester, Minnesota, working with and specializing in treating patients with Parkinson's disease. After leaving the Mayo Clinic, she went on to work in home healthcare for many years, caring for patients with a variety of chronic and acute illnesses as well as orthopedic conditions. Recently, she has become Reiki I certified and has been incorporating Reiki with many of her clients. She enjoys paddle boarding, hiking, swimming, and spending time with her family at the beach.

CHAPTER 23

SOUL SPEAK

COMMUNICATING SOUL TO SOUL WITH YOUR LOVED ONE

Brittani Frey

MY STORY

My eyes were stinging as I fought back the urge to let the tears roll down my face. I was trying my hardest to be strong and not let the emotion overwhelm me. Sitting on my bed, I closed my eyes, focusing on taking deep breaths in and out. Each breath moved through me, allowing my body to become more and more relaxed. I thought, *Brittani, you can do this. You have connected with hundreds of souls before.*

This time was different. I wasn't doing it for a client, rather, I was doing it for my family, the people I love dearly, and I didn't want to get any of it wrong. Of course, I never want to get it wrong, but my emotions can sometimes get in the way when it's family. When I finally felt calm enough, I closed my eyes again and aligned with my higher self. I set the intention that only the highest and best was allowed in my space, and I was ready to connect to this individuals' soul. In deep connection, eyes closed, I spoke out loud, "Tom, if you are here and I have your permission to connect to your soul, please come forward now." In that moment, I felt a shift of energy in the room, almost like a warm, gentle breeze that came across me.

I could feel, by the presence of energy in the room, that Tom was ready to speak soul to soul. I said, "Hi Tom! Thank you for allowing me to connect with you today. I know this may feel a bit different than our other face-to-face encounters. I have a lot of experience communicating and helping souls (in physical and non-physical form) with understanding their journey. I wanted to offer you comfort and peace in your final stages of your human experience." There were a few moments when I thought to myself, *are you there? Are you going to respond?*

He finally replied, "Brit, I knew with my cancer diagnosis that this day would finally come. I am afraid to die. I don't know if I will make it to heaven. What will my loved ones do after I am gone." I knew in that moment that my role would be to provide reassurance and assist him with any soul healing he would work on. A moment later, I felt a cool breeze fill the space in my room. It was December, and I had no windows open. With my eyes closed, I asked that whatever this presence be to please come up closer so I could see more clearly. The souls that had entered were Tom's mom, dad, and brother. I saw them gather around Tom's soul and embrace him in a giant hug. I heard them say, "You are safe, Tom. We will make sure you know that we are here with you every step of the way. We will be waiting for you as your soul leaves your body. It will be a beautiful experience if you trust and allow yourself to have it." It all happened so quickly, yet it was such a powerful moment.

This soul speak conversation I had with Tom was on December 10, 2020, when Tom received the news that his cancer had taken over his body. There were no more treatments left that he could do. His eighteen-month battle with cancer was quickly coming to an end. Tom is my husband's uncle. There were so many moments my husband would say to me, "Why does this have to be happening to Tom? Why does someone who has lived such an amazing life have to go through this?" Throughout Tom's cancer journey I shared multiple times with my husband the experiences that each individual soul chooses. To us, it doesn't always make sense. We cannot change the path a soul chooses to experience. For us, understanding that concept can be rather challenging, especially when it's someone we love so much. It's painful for us to watch, and we wish to do anything possible to help that person.

This can be true for so many different reasons, including when someone is suffering from anxiety or depression, addiction, cancer, the loss of a child, dementia, and so forth. When we can start to see why situations occur on a soul level, we can create awareness that it's all about a soul experience. We want to attach an emotion to it, which is the human perspective. Within my soul sessions, I'm able to help others understand this concept more, allowing my clients to see each situation from a soul level.

It was the first week of February, and as I do each morning, I was sitting in my meditation space. I closed my eyes, took some deep breaths, and centered myself. I heard Tom's voice say, "Brit, I could really use your help now," and away he went. I received no other details from him. Later that evening, my husband received a call from his dad saying that Tom had taken a turn for the worse and they were going to move him to his sister's home. My father-in-law mentioned that they didn't even think he would make it through the night. The next day my husband, sister-in-law, and I went to visit Tom. We were all just floored when we saw him. He was chipper and talking and telling us stories from his life. It seemed as if he got a second wind. My father-in-law was actually stunned by the turnaround Tom made. We didn't stay long as they were expecting a lot of visitors. Before we left, I said to Tom, "Do you mind if I come back another time so we can talk?" I knew it was time we had an in-person conversation.

The morning I was planning my visit with Tom, I felt a sense of apprehension. My nerves were all over the place, literally feeling like my skin was crawling. There were so many thoughts racing through my mind. *What will Tom and the family think of me? They haven't physically seen or experienced "this side of me" yet, the side of me that is filled with wisdom, intuitive gifts and has greatly impacted hundreds of people. Will they think I am nuts?* I had to center myself with some deep breathing and reassure myself that I was going to be okay, that this whole experience was needed not only for Tom and my family but also for myself. Little did I know that what I was about to do would greatly impact everyone on another level. If I had let the ego and my wild thoughts win, the story would have ended here. I want to give you a quick reminder, when the doubt creeps in and the self-judgement is loud, take a leap of faith. Trust yourself and the wisdom you carry. Remind yourself that you're an incredible being with so much to offer those around you.

When I got downstairs to see Tom, he was peacefully sleeping. I mentioned to the family that I would do some soul speak conversation while he was asleep as well as some energy healing. I also mentioned to them that I would love to come upstairs and talk with them once I was through. I settled into a chair next to the bed and closed my eyes, preparing to connect to Tom's soul. As soon as I closed my eyes, I verbally heard Tom say, "Hey Brit! Happy to see you." I opened my eyes and gave Tom a smile. I moved my chair closer to Tom as he was very quiet and physically weak. I jumped right into the question I wanted to ask him. Based on our previous soul conversations about his fear of the afterlife, I asked, "So Tom, where do you think you're headed after this?" His response was, "I sure hope I am making it into heaven." "Without a doubt, Tom, that is where you are going!" I said. He gave me a quirky little smile and said, "Thank goodness." Since he was very weak and tired, that was about the extent of our conversation. I made my way upstairs, where the others were sitting. I explained to them what they could expect to see and experience with Tom, the energetics and spiritual components that go into the death process.

The next morning, I woke up and recalled a dream I had the night before. Tom came to me and showed me that his loved ones surrounded him at his bedside. They were standing around him, joining hand to hand, saying prayers and their final goodbyes. The dream seemed very familiar to me, sort of like a déjà vu, like I'd had this dream before. I did have this dream before. The two nights leading up to my grandma's death, she came to me and showed me this exact thing. Regarding Tom, I never told anyone about my dream because I thought it was just more of a memory from my grandma. I just went about my day, not giving that dream anymore thought.

On February 10, 2021 I had another soul speak session with Tom. That morning I sat on my couch, ready to connect soul to soul. I deeply knew this would be the last soul to soul conversation I was going to have with him before he left his physical body. This time was different. This time I let the emotion flow right through me. There were many tears and yet an overwhelming sense of peace. I heard the laughter and joy waiting for him on the other side of the veil. I heard the clanking of glasses as his mom, dad, and brother saluted his life in a "cheers!" I felt so much weight being lifted physically, mentally, and emotionally.

A few hours later, I asked the family members with him if it would be okay if I stopped by. Within moments of my arrival, his son came upstairs and, in a worrisome tone, said, "Dad's breathing has made a drastic change." All of the family members that were present, gathered around his beside. I went up to Tom, leaned over, and whispered in his ear, "This is it, the moment you have been waiting for. You are surrounded by so much love in this moment. It's time to go home now." There was this heavy sadness that filled the room. Everyone started to move in closer to Tom, and someone said, "should we say a few prayers?" The image of the dream I had a few nights prior popped into my mind. I asked, "Can we please join hands as we do this?" It was a very emotional experience, and within moments, Tom took his last breath. I watched his soul leave his body, guiding and watching him make his way back home, his loved ones on the other side of the veil welcoming him with open arms.

About ten minutes or so after Tom transitioned, my father-in-law said, "Let's have a toast in honor of Tom." We clanked glasses together and said, "Here's to Tom." The clanking of the glasses was the same sound I heard a few months prior in the initial soul speak session I had with Tom. To physically witness this experience left me in complete awe. I never once expressed to the family the clanking of the glasses and the toast to Tom. It naturally occurred and showed me that every human being and experience are woven together, like a tiny piece of thread woven together to create a blanket. Life is like that. When I showed up in those last few moments of Tom's life, I knew I was meant to be there. Like the needle that guides the thread into how it will be woven together, I was weaving the loved ones in spirit with the loved ones left behind. We are all woven together, connected in beautiful and amazing ways.

It was that day, February 10th, that I chose to become a certified death doula. I thank Tom each and every day for giving me the experience to walk alongside him through his last few months. As well as showing me what my purpose and mission here on earth is. When I sat down to write this chapter, I wanted to connect with Tom once again and ask if it would be okay to share his story. In deep connection with his soul again, I heard him reply, "Brit, you guided me out of my pain and suffering and into an experience full of peace and joy. That is a gift and a story you must share with the world."

THE TOOL

Do you want to learn how you can communicate soul-to-soul with a loved one? Remember that you can do this whether the person is still in the physical or has already passed on. I'm going to lead you through a soul speak session so you can communicate with a loved one. This can be done with a loved one who has already died or one who is still currently living. If you would rather listen to the audio version of this, it is available to you at www.healinglovelight.com/resources

Start by finding a comfortable seated position in a space where you will not be interrupted for the next few moments. Take some nice deep breaths in through your nose, followed by an open-mouth exhale. Allow each breath you take, to relax you more and more. As you focus on your breath, imagine your energy being pulled into the core of your body, whether that is your heart or stomach. Within your core is a beam of golden light; as you continue your breath, allow that light to fill each of your cells in your body with this golden light. Now imagine yourself hopping on an elevator; this elevator is taking you higher and higher, past the Universe and galaxy, into a space that is the purest and most magnificent space you have ever been. As the elevator comes to a stop, the door opens, and you take a step out. You start walking along this path.

You begin to notice the vibrant color of the grass, leaves, and flowers. You can smell the most fragrant smell of lilacs and flowers. You can feel the sun beaming down on you, warming your skin with the golden rays. You can hear the beautiful song of the birds welcoming you to this magnificent space. At the end of the path, you notice a bench. You walk up to the bench, taking a seat on the left side. You close your eyes for a moment, taking a few deep breaths, and allow yourself to feel peaceful and so elated to be in this welcoming space. You then take a moment to invite in your loved one that you so deeply want to have a conversation with—asking them, with much love and kindness, to come to sit with you on this beautiful welcoming bench. As they sit next to you, you turn towards them, taking your left hand and placing it on their heart space. You invite them to do the same. As you sit there, facing each other, with your left hands on each other's heart, you just breathe for a few moments. By doing this, you open up the space to start communicating. When the time feels right, you start to share with them everything that has been on your heart, knowing you're both in such a safe and magnificent space to share what you've been so deeply wanting to say. You can spend as much time with them as you would like, knowing that you can come back to this space as often as you wish.

When you feel the conversation is finished, thank your loved one for joining you in this space. Slowly, and when it feels right, leave this space, coming back to the elevator. Take one last look before the door closes and relish in the gratitude of what just occurred. When the door of the elevator closes, make your way back down into your physical body. Returning to deep inhales and exhales. Feel the peace and love that has filled your heart. Know that this experience and practice can be shortened. It is all about having the intention to speak soul to soul, with an open heart, to your loved one. Namaste.

Brittani Frey is a soul whisperer, conscious creator, brilliant manifestor, and death doula. Brittani specializes and deeply understands the soul's journey. Brittani understands just how your beliefs can create fear about your soul self and how to help you understand the truth about your soul's energy. Brittani has worked with hundreds of individuals from all over the globe and through all walks of life. She knows that all human beings have been through some form of trauma that has created fear and resistance around living life aligned with their soul self. Through training in a multitude of healing modalities, she can best support you through life and through death. She knows that most people avoid the topic of death and is here to compassionately support her clients through the process, showing the family how to best support and understand the emotional, physical, and mental components of the dying process. Through coaching, workshops, classes, sessions, and retreats, she provides incredible insight and guidance. Brittani says, "I am here to change the dynamic fear of death and bring in more understanding and compassion." Brittani is also the mother to two amazing boys, married to her soul mate, and enjoys traveling and being in nature. For more information or to contact Brittani, please visit www.healinglovelight.com

CHAPTER 24

THE ART OF LETTING GO

THERE IS NOTHING TO FEAR BUT FEAR ITSELF

Pamela Schneider

MY STORY

When I was young, death seemed so scary. It felt so final.

As a little girl, I didn't quite understand when my grandfather died; it felt like a bad thing to no longer have him in my life.

As more relatives fell ill and passed away, and time went on, I learned to come to peace with them leaving the physical plane.

But I was still afraid of losing the people I loved and of dying myself because I didn't know what happened when you die.

When my father took his own life, I was just a girl of fifteen. It felt so final; I felt so abandoned. My grieving went on for decades.

It wasn't until I was in my late thirties and living with a man who had a dog that became ill that I was able to experience how death is truly a transition to a pure, blissful energy.

Her name was Piddles, a beautiful strawberry blond golden retriever. By the time I came along, she was already thirteen years old, so I started to call her Mrs. Piddles; it felt more fitting.

I was quite ill myself at the time with migraines, anxiety, and depression, so I was home a lot with Mrs. Piddles, and we became good friends. She was always with me, following me room to room and even into the bathroom when it was time for me to go.

One day we noticed what looked like a wart on her face. We immediately took her to have it checked out and were told it was not a big deal. This spot started to grow quickly, though, and we became concerned because golden retrievers are known for having cancerous spots like this.

We visited vet after vet, who refused to remove it because of her age. This saddened and enraged me. She was otherwise so healthy and could have lived for so much longer if they would just remove it!

Time went on, a full year where it grew on her face, but she still had a good quality of life. Until it got to the point where it was so big, it started to twist up her face and nose, and one day she started to spit up puddles of blood.

It was scary to see her in pain, pools of blood coming out of her mouth. But, she handled it with so much grace. I did my best to keep my cool and not panic when it would happen and do what I could to keep her comfortable.

We brought her to the vet again, at the Cape where we were staying. The vet, a wonderful local woman who truly loved animals, tested her blood and shared with us that she was at a point where she was dying, and there was no coming back from it. It was time to put her to sleep so she would no longer suffer.

We knew this was coming for quite some time, but it was still hard to process.

I could not bear to see her in pain, so I knew it was what needed to be done.

We set a time for the vet to come to our house the next day and started to dig a hole in the garden and collect things we loved to create a memorial for her.

The next day came. It was a beautiful and sunny late spring day. We set a blanket outside by the edge of the forest; you could hear the sounds of the ocean in the distance. The air smelled sweet. As I sat down and put her head on my lap, I thought about how grateful I was to have such a magical place, such a beautiful, peaceful setting for her to transition. I had no idea what would happen beyond what I was told, that it would be peaceful and quick. I knew I needed to stay calm and focus on keeping her comfortable.

I whispered soft words of reassurance to her, petting her ears, "You're going to cross over now. We'll be together in spirit."

The vet gave her an IV, and she slipped into a dream state.

I thought that was going to be it.

And then I saw the most beautiful golden orb rise out of her body and towards the sun. First, my mind wanted to think I was hallucinating, but then my body was filled with an overwhelmingly strong, blissful energy that felt like the purest unconditional love I have ever felt.

This energy was so beautiful and so powerful it brought tears of joy to my eyes. All of my thoughts ceased to exist, and I was totally present, bathing in this energy.

I sat for a while as my entire being was vibrating with blissful source energy. It was such a beautiful experience. This energy was like nothing I've ever felt before. From that moment on, I could feel that death was not a scary thing. I then knew that death was a returning to pure source energy, an energy so pure and clean that nothing scary could possibly live there.

If this is what dying felt like, I was alright with it. This energy felt so good that I longed to touch it again and experience it running through my body one more time. I knew I had to share this story with others, so they could understand that death is a beautiful thing, not to be feared. And as I traveled further along the path of my spiritual journey, I realized that to be able to live fully, I needed to face my fear of death.

So when the opportunity to write this chapter came along, I knew I had to be a part of it. If we want to truly live our lives fully while we're here, we need to reframe what death means to us so we can let go of any fear we have about dying.

If death is such a beautiful experience, why do those who are left behind have such a hard time with it?

It seems the thing that causes us the most suffering when it comes to death is that we get attached to the idea of what having someone in our life means to us. We project this idea into the future and expect that they will always be there. Learning to let go of that seems to be the hardest part.

Shortly after Mrs. Piddle's passing, I consulted a psychic medium to connect with all of my loved ones that had passed. "Your father is often sitting right beside you," she said, "You can meditate and connect with him whenever you want to." She also told me that I had the spirit of a dog with me, and I hadn't told her about Mrs. Piddles.

What beautiful confirmation.

I decided to give the meditation thing a try, and when I closed my eyes and set the intention to connect with him, I was brought to a tree in a field by the edge of the woods. He was sitting under the tree, and we had a conversation where I shared everything I've ever wanted to say.

A month later, when I was visiting my mom, I shared this with her, and she gasped and told me that she meditated to connect with him as well, and she always meets him under a tree, in a field, on the edge of the woods, it sounded like the same place I described.

Knowing that our loved ones are always with us, and we can communicate with them, along with the experience of the energy of what crossing over feels like, helped me fully come to terms with and reframe my ideas about death. It didn't feel like such a permanent loss, and I knew that the energy of what is on the other side is so beautiful, I was at peace with my loved ones going there.

This all lead me to create The Art of Letting Go to share my medicine for what helps me to move through strong emotions and come to a place of acceptance and peace.

THE TOOL

THE ART OF LETTING GO

Gather a playlist of your favorite music, download or cue up *Cello drone in D* from youtube, get together your favorite art supplies (I love watercolor paint but you can use whatever you have or whatever excites you) and set aside two hours for this sacred space of self-expression. If you'd like, light some candles, or burn some sage or incense.

This is your time to let it all out, hold yourself, express yourself, and let yourself be with whatever wants to come up.

There are no wrong emotions, feelings, movements, sounds, or pen or brush strokes.

Sit and close your eyes. Drop into your body and feel your breath breathing you. Take your awareness from your head to your heart.

Now set an intention for what you want to let go of. Maybe it's the attachment you have to a person, maybe it's heavy feelings, maybe it's something else. Take this intention and place it in your heart and expand your heart energy out so big that it's bigger than your body, the room you're in, the house you're in, the state you're in, the entire world. Expand it out so it's touching the entire Universe, all things, and the space between all things.

Now ask your heart. How is this serving me? Your system is incredibly wise, and everything you experience serves you in some way. Don't judge it; just observe. Ask your heart, are you willing to let this go now? The answer may be no, and that's okay. Reassure your heart that it's safe to let go. It's time to let go. In life, we do not need to push things away. We simply need to decide that we're done with them and then trust they will fade away as we go about living. Decide now that this is what is happening as you sing, paint, dance, and live. When you're ready, come back to the room. Wiggle your fingers and toes, open your eyes. Stretch and move as you're guided.

Now turn on the cello drone, loud enough so that you feel the music reverberating through your body. Close your eyes and drop your awareness back into your heart. Take a few deep breaths. Remember, there are no wrong sounds. Picture your entire body as an instrument. FEEL the music.

Now open your mouth and let whatever sounds want to come out come out. Raw and unfiltered, this is a way to practice surrendering more deeply and trusting yourself more. Let yourself explore this for the entire song, at least eight minutes so that you have a chance to really drop into the discomfort and let go.

Once you have finished this part, cue up your favorite playlist of music, about five songs or at least 20 minutes (Find my favorite playlist here: https://www.thetemplewithin.us/art-of-letting-go). Stand up. Close your eyes and drop into your body, your breath, and your heart. FEEL the music reverberating throughout your body. Let the music move your body however it wants to move. There are no wrong movements. Everything is welcome here. You may feel emotions and cry, or get angry; let it all be what it is and don't judge it. In this sacred space, all is welcome. It's all good. Keep dancing and moving and letting your body be moved, be free until the music ends. Keep your eyes closed and stay connected with your body; if you find you're overthinking, come back to stillness and re-connect with your body. When the music ends, take a moment to sit and reflect on this experience. Do you feel you fully let yourself be moved?

Now it is time to paint. We are fully trusting that what needed to move through you and release has happened. Now it's time to set an intention for what you want to create going forward. Set this intention now, and we're going to create an energetically encoded piece of art that will carry the energy of this intention so that while it's in your space and whenever you look at it, the energy of this intention will continue to work on you.

Get your art supplies arranged so they're easy to reach. Put your paper in front of you and then close your eyes, drop into your body, breath, and heart, and see your new intention expanding out into the Universe. There is no need to have a pre-determined idea of what you will create. This is surrendered painting (or drawing). The goal is to trust what's coming through and not overthink it. Now open your eyes and let your hands do what they want to. Let what wants to come through, come through. Try not to think about it; you're being guided by spirit. There are no wrong brush strokes here. Let spirit move through you and create what wants to be created. If you start to overthink, close your eyes and drop back into your body, heart, and breath. You will reach the point where it feels complete, or you may even be told to stop. Listen to this guidance. You may receive guidance about what the different parts of your creation mean or a deeper meaning behind your intention. Let it come. And if none comes, that's okay too.

Now sit and reflect on this experience. What did you feel when you were painting? How do you feel now?

You can come back to these practices for fun or whenever you feel strong emotions or want to move energy and process something. Sometimes you may be rage dancing. Sometimes it might be to cry. Or both. Whatever it is, this is a powerful way to explore deeper levels of surrender, release, and self-trust. It's a practice in embodying more self-love and acceptance. It will help re-wire your nervous system, and it's great for your inner child.

Pamela Schneider was born in Springfield, Massachusetts, and grew up in Western Massachusetts. She spent her 20s and 30s trying to find her purpose and worked in many different fields. She became ill while living in New York City and attending Columbia University and moved home to Massachusetts to try to heal. She'd tried many different traditional western treatments and was not making any progress, until she met her grandmother's friend at her funeral and learned she had been a doctor in a hospital with "no machines, no medicines, JUST FOOD!" Fascinated, she began reading more about this and changed her diet. Within two months, most of her physical ailments went away. After spending two years tapering off of the medications she'd been relying on, she felt called to help others make healthy changes in their lives and enrolled at the Institute for Integrative Nutrition's Health Coaching Program to study holistic healing, nutritional healing, and coaching. After graduating from the program, which brought her through a messy divorce from an abusive relationship feeling more balanced and whole than she'd ever been before, she still felt like there was more to healing. Feeling drawn to reiki and energy work, she began her Usui Reiki certification and quickly progressed through the levels to master. Fascinated by the shifts that energy work can create for her clients, Pamela continued her education to include Kundalini Reiki, The Akashic Records, the Goddess Ascension Codes, and The Emotion Code. Pamela now works with clients combining these modalities to create massive shifts in their lives. She is also a High Priestess who works with other women walking the path to their power and shows people how to create the life they've dreamed of and experience big life transitions like birth and death with grace.

For more information or to contact Pamela, please visit at www.thetemplewithin.us

CHAPTER 25

FILLING YOUR EMPTY CUP

SELF-CARE FOR THOSE HARDWIRED TO GIVE

James Kealiipiilani Kawainui, Native Hawaiian Healer,
Spiritual Counselor, and kahu (priest)

MY STORY

I'm hardwired to take care of people. It's been that way since I was a child. Being the oldest of eight naturally put me in that position. I had a tendency in the past to take on too much because I didn't know how to say no. Whenever anyone needed help, I was there, the knight in shining armor, swooping in to save the day. I gave away my energy like it was a limitless source.

It took me years to realize why I did it. I had an agenda I wasn't aware of; a deep need to be wanted, valued, relevant, and loved. It was something I felt I never got growing up. I've spent most of my life searching for appreciation and acceptance.

It's one of the reasons I got into the relationship that took me to New Zealand.

I somehow knew I was going to New Zealand long before I was invited to go. I also knew I would be there for a while, though at the time, I didn't understand why. We were going for three months, and I was along for the ride.

In my experience with my clients over the years, I noticed that as humans we constantly compromise ourselves and make decisions based on survival. My time in New Zealand was definitely based on that. I was in a country where I didn't know many people, and was visiting on a tourist visa. If the situation went to shit, I wouldn't have many options. Our tickets were one-way, bought by Stacy, my girlfriend of only two months. And, oh yeah, I had little money of my own. *Not a good plan, James!* I had to make sure that whatever happened, I wasn't going to get tossed out on my ass. Years later, upon reflection, I saw that if I made myself indispensable, I could stay in New Zealand on my own, should the need arise.

After we arrived, I met Stacy's family. Her parents, JT and Sarah, were a beautiful couple, married for over 60 years, still living on their own in the home they had built together years before. Karen was the middle sister, Lisa the oldest. Besides being family, what bonded them together was a fierce independent streak and a high level of stubbornness. These, I came to learn, are very New Zealand traits.

Over the next few months, I poured my energy into this family, jumping in to help wherever I could. "I am going to do whatever it takes to make you like me" was a strategy I had developed over the years, so of course, I used it here.

The reality was that the parents, or "The Olds," as they were called, really did need help. No one in the family had taken the time to notice, mainly because they weren't there day in and day out. JT was 92 years old, not as mobile or handy as he had been in his younger years. He'd built airfields for the Allied forces during WWII and had spent his career as an engineer for the Ministry, building hydroelectric plants across both the North and South Islands. He was full of stories, and I would sit transfixed for hours listening to him recount his glory years.

Sarah was 86 and every bit the prim and proper English woman. She arrived by steamship to New Zealand in the early 20th century with her parents as a teenager of 16. She ran her house like a well-oiled machine. Everything had its place. Meals were at the same time every day (and you did not want to be late!). She never worked outside of home her entire life and had lived an insular life.

Months went by. Three turned into six, then into nine. We kept extending our trip, and I slowly became absorbed in the family's daily life, still unsure why I was there. My partner and I moved into the flat next door in a house owned by her dad. I borrowed a wetsuit and started surfing again. Surfing has always been a very important part of my life from a very young age. It's the place I felt most at home and at peace. Karen's daughter and her partner surfed and would come by, pick me up, and zip me off to a new spot. The waves in New Zealand were some of the best I had surfed in my life. It's an amazingly beautiful country. I was hungry for adventure and took the liberty of going out to explore as often as I could.

When we weren't out exploring, we were with her parents. I began to notice that things were in various states of disrepair. "I've been meaning to get to that," was JT's favorite reply. After a while, not having much else to do, I discreetly started "tidying up."

As I began to do more, the projects grew larger. I knew it was time to have a conversation with JT. I needed his buy-in. "I was noticing that it's a bit of a challenge getting to the coal box and woodpile in the garage, and I wouldn't want Sarah to trip over anything and get hurt." "I think a good tidy-up is in order," he replied. "Well," I said, "How about I pop down to the hardware store and pick up a few bags of coal?" And so it went, and the project list was born.

I was beginning to understand the family dynamics in play. Karen lived outside the city on a small farm that kept her busy. Lisa's anger and cynicism were always palpable. She took to stopping by to see her parents when we weren't there. The only thing that bound the sisters together was their parents. And even in that, they often disagreed. Conversations were short and clipped, at best.

There was mounting suspicion from Karen and Lisa of my growing involvement with their parents. They didn't know or trust me, and as the months went by, they were watching their parents rely more and more on me for help. They were convinced their parents didn't need it. I was certain they were a bit annoyed as I became a frequent topic of conversation about what I was doing around the house. They hadn't noticed their parents' slow decline because they weren't there to notice it.

They had their own lives and had taken a hands-off approach years earlier. Karen lived outside the city and came in just to see friends. She would pop over for the occasional cup of tea or dinner with "The Olds." Lisa was a little more involved in their lives, doing the weekly grocery shopping. Other than that, their parents had been left to live their lives.

In the midst of all this, Stacy decided she had to go back to Hawaii, afraid she would lose her green card status. She booked her ticket and was gone in a week. Now I was alone, in a county where I knew exactly eight people, having met practically no one in the year I'd been there. *What have I got myself into?* There was nothing to do but dive deeper into the role of caregiver that I'd created for myself. I was energetically supporting two elderly people I barely knew, whose family wasn't sure whether to trust me or send me packing. *I have to try harder and take on more.*

Over the next six months, I settled into a routine with "The Olds." Every day, I was providing assistance, working on the various projects I had going, and slowly bringing the house and garden back into shape. My "partner" fell completely off the radar. She called, maybe once a week, for just a few minutes. *Not much of a relationship.* I had no income but no real expenses. I picked up a few handyman gigs on the side for gas money, so I could go surfing and the occasional flat white coffee. The reality was I had nowhere else to go and nothing calling me back to Hawaii. Plus, because of all the time we were spending together, I was growing quite fond and protective of "The Olds." I came to the slow realization that I was there to help them both get ready to cross over.

I *wasn't* aware of how much of my energy I was giving away the longer I took care of them. By this point, all the sisters were perfectly happy to hand over the responsibility of caring for their parents. It meant they could go on with their lives uninterrupted. I knew I was taking on too much, but I did it anyway. My pattern of giving myself away was in full swing.

Eventually, I hit the wall. It took about two and a half years, which in hindsight, was crazy. It became too overwhelming, and I was drained, physically and emotionally. As much as I wanted to, I couldn't keep going. Believe me, I tried! Stacy had come back from Hawaii by then, and there was no way we would be able to do this without assistance. It had become a 24 hour a day job. We even employed a baby monitor up at the flat, which we kept by the bed in case of nocturnal emergencies. That contributed to less sleep which wore us out even more. There was less and less "me time" and ultimately no time at all. It was all-encompassing. Despite everything, I tried to keep going.

The sisters finally got involved and stepped in to help a few months before Sarah passed. JT passed 18 months later. They died at home, peacefully, their wishes fulfilled, surrounded by loved ones. These were four extremely stressful yet rewarding years.

It wasn't until I met my spiritual teacher (also while I was in New Zealand) that I learned how to care for others without it affecting me personally. It took another ten years before I learned about healthy boundaries, how to say no, and to be okay with that inside of myself.

*****

How many of you are caregivers who, for whatever reason, are giving too much and not taking enough time for yourself? Here are some statistics to consider.

- Up to 70% of people who are caregivers suffer from some form of depression.
- 60% of caregivers consider themselves in poor health.
- About six in ten caregivers in a national survey reported that their eating (63%) and exercising (58%) habits were worse than before.
- And perhaps most shocking of all, 30% of caregivers die before the person they are caring for.

SELF-CARE IS A NON-NEGOTIABLE!

Not taking care of yourself is a recipe for disaster. Ask yourself, "What is the impact my caregiving has on me, physically, emotionally, mentally, and spiritually?" How often do I give myself away? Working long hours, driving myself to exhaustion, and continuously putting myself at the bottom of the list is not a good model for self-care. Neither is not being able to ask for help.

As much as you may think you can do it all by yourself, the truth is you can't, and you shouldn't be. Nothing is more important than your health and wellbeing. Just remember, you can't give from an empty cup! The long-term negative consequences of not taking care of yourself are too great. I've seen it too many times in my own life and in the lives of the people I've worked with over the years.

If you find yourself in this position, here are some questions to contemplate that may help you get clear about where you are inside of yourself right now. I invite you to look underneath the surface and *explore the real reasons behind why you are doing what you are doing.* Not only in your role as caregiver but how you are living your life in general.

Take some time to journal these questions:

- What are the motives driving my choices to be an overachieving, overworked caregiver?
- Is it really out of the goodness of my heart and love for the person?
- Are there other factors at play I haven't or won't admit to myself?
- Am I doing this from a sense of obligation or guilt?
- Are my actions originating from a need to be acknowledged, appreciated, or loved?
- Is the reason financial, because me or my family simply can't afford to get proper help?
- Am I harboring anger and resentment for having to put my life on hold or having to walk away from a career or significant relationship?

Giving yourself time and space to answer these questions honestly is a first step towards self-care.

And here is a practice you can use to help you go even further.

*AUTHORS NOTE: Names were changed to honor the privacy of the people in this story.

THE TOOL

SELF-CARE FOR THOSE HARDWIRED TO GIVE

For caregivers of any capacity, the need for some kind of daily meditation practice cannot be overemphasized. A consistent daily meditation practice has been scientifically proven to:

- significantly reduce stress
- lower the chance of heart disease
- reduce the symptoms of insomnia
- help regulate anxiety, and
- slow the aging process

Just to name a few.

How often do you give yourself time to settle your energy, get quiet, and set your intention for the day, as well as for your life? *Any answer less than every day is unacceptable!* It's impossible to be a caregiver if you're not taking care of yourself, period. Taking time for a centering healing meditation can be as short as five to ten minutes. Even as busy as your life is, **you are worth ten minutes of your time every day.**

Here is a practice I not only use myself but have shared many times over the years with the people I've worked with. This is not intended as the be-all and end-all. Consider this a starting point and expand and adapt it as you get more comfortable.

If you already have a daily practice, that's awesome. There may still be something in here that will enhance what you're doing or be a simple reminder. Either way, you can't lose.

A free audio recording is available at:
www.jameskawainui.com/selflovetimeoutmeditation

Find or create a quiet space for yourself where you won't be interrupted. Be sure to give yourself sufficient time, so you don't run off right after you're done. Turn off your cell phone or leave it in another room where you won't hear it. You can do with a phone break for a few minutes!

If it helps, light a candle. There is something deeply soothing about a candle. Take a few moments to gaze at the candle and create an intention to give whatever it is you are holding onto to the flame as you go through your meditation.

Gently close your eyes and slowly become aware of your breath. Focusing on your breath will always help bring you into a state of calmness.

See and sense your breath as you begin to focus, feeling the air as it passes through your nose, travels down the back of your throat, and fills your lungs. Notice the sensation of your chest rising and falling as you breathe. Your breath becomes your only thought, permeating your awareness. If a thought about your day, the person you are caring for, or that gallon of milk you need from the store comes in, see it, and give yourself permission to let it go and return to focusing on your breath. Let your full attention be only on the act and feeling of breathing.

Notice if there are changes in your body as you breathe. If your mind wants to take over, notice the thoughts, then let them go. Instead, turn your mind to this thought; *I love and care about myself so much that I am taking these precious few minutes to focus on my breath, body, and how I feel. Doing this is an act of self-love, and I am grateful.*

If it feels right to you, say a short prayer. I call out and thank the Divine Source (God, Buddha, Jesus, Allah, Mother Mary, whatever that is for you). I ask for guidance as I go through my day. "Let me be a better person today than I was yesterday" is something I always affirm.

Call in your guides, guardians, and angels and ask them for assistance as you move through your day.

"Let my day flow gracefully, so there is all the time to accomplish everything that needs to be done."

Find two or three things in your life you are grateful for. They don't have to be grandiose. The more gratitude you allow into your life, the more you'll see and find things to be grateful for as your day goes on. Feeling grateful then becomes a simple pause in your day, however brief, that will help slow you down, so you don't feel as if you're rushing from one thing to the next.

Add anything else that may come to mind or anything you feel guided to do as you take this special "me time."

Consistently setting your day like this will change how you go through it. I know it sounds simple, but I've seen it work time and again. My clients comment how differently their day is when they *don't* take the time to set their intentions for the day.

This is "you-taking-care-of-you" in this one small way. It is a precious act of self-love and kindness. It is more than okay to do this.

You are special, you are loved, and you deserve it.

James Kawainui is a Native Hawaiian Healer with deep family roots in ancient Hawaii. Over Twenty years ago, James walked away from the "corporate world" and moved back to Hawaii. Since then, he has lived, studied, and worked with Traditional Hawaiian and New Zealand Maori Healers. James is the creator of a modern energy healing technique based on both ancient wisdom and modern medicine, designed to facilitate deep transformation. The effects are life-changing and help to reset the body to its Innate Natural Wisdom.

Results are often described as miraculous by his clients and often include:

- Permanent reduction and/or elimination of chronic or ongoing physical and emotional pain.

- Significant reduction of stress, emotional trauma, depression, and the effects of PTSD.

- Identification and clearing of generational and ancestral emotional and behavioral patterns.

- Restoration of *Your Mana* and the natural energetic flow of your body for optimum health and wellbeing.

- Re-establishing your Spiritual connection to **Source Energy** and Your Higher Self.

James routinely works with people from many cultures and countries through his remote healing work.

James speaks to many organizations and groups, teaching classes on Hawaiian Spirituality, mindfulness, meditation, and energy healing. He has a comprehensive mentoring program for practitioners and health care professionals that covers components of grounding, understanding of energetic boundaries, and the development of an elevated spiritual practice.

James offers free 30-minute consultations:

> https://jameskawainui.com/get-back-on-track/

For information on scheduling a session, speaking engagements, podcasts, or classes, contact James:

> Email: kahu457@gmail.com

> Website: http://jameskawainui.com/

FollowJames:

Facebook: https://www.facebook.com/jameskawainui/

Instagram: https://www.instagram.com/jameskawainui/

YouTube:
https://m.youtube.com/channel/UCBLNjzVMSDhaWX3NxMPNTzA

MY PERSONAL ACKNOWLEDGEMENTS

My forever gratitude to Ramesh Manian, my husband and anchor, who supports me through my endless, ever-changing endeavors. Thank you for reading my early drafts, giving me advice, and making sure the kids stayed on track with schoolwork and didn't miss their activities. I couldn't have done this without you.

My greatest thanks to my beautiful daughter, Reha, and my loving son, Aryan. I learn so much from you every day. I appreciate your patience, constant encouragement, support, love, and hugs.

I am in immense gratitude to the village that loves, supports, and surrounds me.

To my dearest mom Bharati, thank you for being the wind beneath my wings, my strength, and my grounding. Thank you for sharing your endless wisdom and experiences with me. I truly appreciate all that you do for my family and me.

To my dad, who watches over me from the heavens. Thank you for starting me on this journey and for your continued guidance, signs, and nudges to keep me on my path.

To my siblings, Krupa and Hiren, their better halves, Michael and Pamela, and my nephews, Vihaan, Ayaan, Kyan, and niece, Ariana, I offer gratitude for keeping me in check and entertaining me, always. Thanks for always being present in my life, for loving me unconditionally, and for grounding me.

My deepest thanks to Shelley Astrof for being my calm and putting a smile on my face. I have immense gratitude for your wisdom and your teachings of Bhagavad Gita, for bringing me back to my knower, my soul—the unborn, pure, free, forever, immortal existence.

My heartfelt gratitude to Shraddha Pawar for spending hours listening to me talk about this project and death and dying on our numerous walks and for helping me edit the chapter.

Karen Tasto, thank you so much for inspiring me to be on the amazing adventure of being a Death Doula. Thank you for introducing me to Laura Di Franco at Brave Healer Productions. I am so grateful for your continuous love, support and help with this book.

Amy Gillespie Dougherty, I am beyond grateful to you for your continuous encouragement, motivation and assistance throughout this book process. Thank you for being my cheerleader.

My profound appreciation to Laura Di Franco, for getting me started on this journey of authorship. For guiding me, inspiring me, motivating me, and making my dreams come true.

My heartfelt gratitude to family, friends and mentors who have supported and encouraged me throughout my life. Your guidance and insight help me in my quest to make the world more loving, accepting and compassionate place. Thank you for cheering me on, I wouldn't be here without your support and belief in me.

AN OVERFLOW
OF GRATITUDE

I want to purposefully close this book with the energy of gratitude and grace in hopes that you'll read this last page and imagine all the people in your own life you're grateful for, maybe even some of these fantastic authors!

A word of gratitude to my many patients and clients who allowed me the opportunity to learn through their physical therapy and energy healing experiences. Their love and openness have assisted me in honing my metaphysical skills and expanding my inner gifts.

My thanks go out to God and the spirit of this vision. Thank you to my guides, angels, and light people who've guided me along this journey. There has been tremendous Divine force and energy behind this book, and words can't express the deep pool of overwhelming gratitude I feel in my heart as these words, the words of twenty-five authors, come into print.

A huge, heartfelt thanks to Brave Healer Productions and Laura Di Franco for her amazing vision and guidance and immense patience with me in dealing with my newbie mistakes in bringing this first collaborative book to publication.

To the team at Brave Healer Productions, including publishing assistant, Alex Nason, and our designer, Dino Marino, thank you for making this amazing book as beautiful as the words inside its chapters! You are the unsung heroes of this book, crafting and cleaning our words, pages, and cover.

To our front cover artist, Theodora Elena Engelhart, I'm immensely grateful to our angels, who conspired for us to meet in a far-off land just to bring this vision to life. Thank you for giving this book its face for the world. You turned my idea into a masterpiece. And your gorgeous art has the energy of healing I'd dreamed of when I envisioned the book. Find Theodora at www.risingroots.at

TO EACH AND EVERY ONE OF OUR AUTHORS, thank you for being vulnerable and sharing your painful experiences of loss, moments of shift, and amazing gifts. You touch countless lives with all you do as a resource of transformation. Thank you for saying yes to bringing your amazing gifts, tools, and resources to our readers. You are the power within these pages, and I dearly trust and am in awe of your work, visions, and tools to change the narrative of death, grief, life, and living. Your willingness to share your perspectives, along with your mission to leave our world a better place, inspire and uplift us all. Your willingness to participate in the journey of *Sacred Death* is now written in the super-conscious of our universe. Thank You!

To all our friends, family, colleagues, acquaintances, and book launch team members who supported us during the writing, publishing, launching, and promoting of this project, thank you so much for your support, love, words of encouragement, and purchases. This village is powerful.

HUGE GRATITUDE TO YOU, OUR READER. You've taken a bold step to reach out, go deep into your pain, and learn new ways to be. I applaud you for not only seeking answers beyond death and the meaning of life but actually taking this first step in exploring new tools to do so. By creating a loving, peaceful, and joy-filled world for yourself, you create the same world for everyone around you—my deepest gratitude and thanks.

ABOUT THE AUTHOR

Hemali V. Vora, MPT, is an expert holistic practitioner, intuitive energy healer, and spiritual mentor. With over two decades of working in the healthcare field as a physical therapist, she has helped, coached, and guided hundreds of patients and their families to deal with chronic illnesses, disabilities, and personal traumas.

Hemali is an avid traveler and lifelong learner. Her intuitive guidance, experiences, and curiosity led her to learn many modalities like Myofascial Release, Integrative Nutrition, and Holy Fire & Karuna Reiki. By going through her journey, filled with immense grief, depression, traumas, and health challenges, she taps into her abundant toolbox and integrates into her work. Hemali empowers clients to discover and embody their unique version of optimal mental, emotional, physical, and spiritual health, allowing them to thrive and reach their greatest potential. She often speaks and is hosted at city and local government facilities on programs related to goal setting, nutrition, and the importance of self-care to counter caregiver's burn-out, overwhelm, and stress.

Hemali has taught all levels of Reiki courses to healthcare workers, caregivers, and children to help them uncover their true gifts and talents. Her fascination with every aspect of life, death, and dying inspired her to complete the End of Life Doula training through the University of Vermont, Larner College of Medicine. She provides comprehensive support, comfort, and guidance to dying clients and their families with end-of-life transitions, legacy projects, preparations, and through the bereavement process. She educates communities on the importance of advanced-care planning for end-of-life to achieve comfort and peace. She hosts virtual and online Death Café's, a space to talk about death and dying.

Through her energy and doula work, she has coached many caregivers who accompanied their loved ones experiencing terminal illness and death. Hemali offers one-on-one and group sessions in her studio and through online webinars.

Hemali offers free 30 min consultations, to schedule go to:
www.hemalivora.com

For information on scheduling for workshops, sessions, podcasts or speaking engagements email Hemali at www.hemalivora1@gmail.com

Follow Hemali:
www.facebook.com/coachhemali
www.instagram.com/_happy_healthy_u
www.youtube.com/c/HealingCorner

Hemali has co-authored the latest Amazon bestsellers:

The Ultimate Guide To Self-Healing Techniques

Chapter 10: Mindful Eating: Using Food As Medicine.

Hemali takes us through her kid's and her health struggles and shows us how we all can heal from any illness or trauma through proper nutrition, movement, body energy work, and spiritual work. In addition, she provides a beautiful guided mindful eating exercise to slow down and have a healthy and loving relationship with our food.

The Ultimate Guide To Self-Healing, Volume 4

Chapter 20: Legacy Work: Living Life With Intention And Purpose

In this chapter, Hemali guides you through creating a legacy project, life review, and journey of self-discovery. She helps you with a blueprint for living, making a difference, and connecting your life to a bigger story, to inspire you to start your legacy work while you are living.

SACRED DEATH COURSE
Finding Meaning In Life,
Living In Awareness With Intention And Purpose
Being Prepared For The Inevitable

- Are you anxious or fearful of your death or your loved ones death?

- Are these fears preventing you from living your life to the fullest?

- Are you ready to change your relationship with death and life?

- Are you ready to dive deeper into your authentic life?

The goal of this course is to change your perspective about death and dying, to talk openly about death and all that surrounds it. This is also to help you navigate through the root cause of these fears, make you aware of them, provide you with tools and exercises to courageously assess and move through them with love and compassion.

Start living in the present moment with grace, peace and joy.

Each week we will cover such topics as meditation, journaling, writing obituary, creating Legacy, learning to live in the now, with awareness, purpose and intention.

For more information visit: www.hemalivora.com

ॐ असतो मा सद्गमय ।
तमसो मा ज्योतिर्गमय ।
मृत्योर्मा अमृतं गमय ।
ॐ शान्तिः शान्तिः शान्तिः ॥

Om, Asato maa sad-gamaya

Tamaso maa jyotir-gamaya

mrityorma amritam-gamaya

Om shanti, shanti, shanti

Lead me from the asat (untruth-illusion, duality)

To the sat (truth-True Self-bliss consciousness, non-duality).

Lead me from darkness-ignorance to light,
knowledge of our true nature, Self-Realization

Lead me from death to immortality

Om Peace Peace Peace.